SKYRAIDER

The Douglas A-1 "Flying Dump Truck"

SKYRAIDER

The Douglas A-1 "Flying Dump Truck"

by
Rosario Rausa

 The Nautical & Aviation Publishing Company
Charleston, South Carolina

Library of Congress Catalog Card Number: 99-059319
ISBN: 0-933852-31-2

Library of Congress Cataloging-in-Publication Data:

Rausa, Rosario
        Skyraider: The Douglas A-1 "Flying Dump Truck"

        Bibliography: p.
        1. Skyraider (Fighter planes) I. Title
UG1242.F5 R38 1982 358.4'3 82-14187
ISBN 0-933852-31-2

Second Printing, 1987
Third Printing, 2001
Printed in the United States of America.

Book design by Charissa Maynard.
Jacket paintings by R.G. Smith.

For information on R.G. Smith art, contact Sharlyn Marsh,
315 Montana Street, #108, Santa Monica, CA 90403

To Ed Heinemann,
the Genius of El Segundo

Contents

Preface

The Able Dog served America for more than twenty years. It had such a successful and illustrious life, in and out of combat, that it undeniably deserves its place on the honor roll of superlative flying machines. Volumes could not do it justice. Surely the hundreds upon hundreds who designed, built, maintained, and flew it would agree to that. I make no pretense, therefore, that this is a definitive book about the A-1 Skyraider.

I was lucky to fly the Able Dog for several years in the Navy and am grateful to be among the confraternity of aviators who have climbed in behind that R-3350, fired it up, and roared into the air fully confident that they were driving a winner. I also had the good fortune to befriend Ed Heinemann, "Mr. Attack Aviation," the guiding force behind the conception and development of the Skyraider. Clearly, this spirited, determined man and his skilled associates instilled in the attack bomber a quality of workmanship that is unsurpassed in the world of aviation, past and present.

Through the years few words of ridicule or criticism were hurled at the Skyraider. Oh, it was cursed now and then, to be sure. More than one flyer inveighed against the machine for sending him off the runway into a cloud of dust even though the fault lay with him for not properly counteracting with rudder the horrendous torque that was an Able Dog trademark. Estrangements between pilot and plane existed but were usually brief in duration. And there were few divorces.

Several excellent books profile in detail the aircraft, its progression through a phenomenal seven major versions and twenty-eight subversions, and its operational history. This effort, on the other hand, is intended as neither a chronological nor a technical description of the Spad. Rather, I have tried to capture the essence—or at least a part of the essence—of the relationship between this reliable warrior and those who knew it.

Hopefully, the reader will accept a tendency to embellish a sea story here and there. (Skyraider as well as naval aviation afficionados, in general, will understand such bravado.) I apologize softly for same while admitting that this is a prejudiced account. The Skyraider, propeller and all, was an airplane of enduring strength that held its own even among the jets and did its job right to the end. It's terribly difficult not to be biased in favor of a marvelous aircraft that more than any other was deserving of the title, be it intended for official designation purposes or not, of the *A-1*.

Ed Heinemann in his den at Rancho Santa Fe, California.

Introduction

The best testimony to an aircraft's reputation comes from the pilots who fly it. If they say its good, it follows that the aircraft performed as it was supposed to, if not better. Over the years I've been on the receiving end of many compliments by aviators and other folks extolling the virtues of the Skyraider. It is most gratifying, therefore, to realize that the A-1 was a success.

I consider these endorsements a credit to the American aviation industry and, in particular, to the El Segundo Division of Douglas Aircraft in the post–World War II years. From the engineers to the assembly line work force, we had a talented group dedicated to turning out a quality product. The Skyraider was certainly an example of that. At the time, of course, we couldn't envision that the Able Dog would stay on the scene for nearly three decades. The wars in Korea and Vietnam certainly had something to do with its longevity. Still, the airplane's ability to endure well into the age of jets speaks for itself. It's been an honor to have been associated with such a wonderful flying machine.

However, the pilots and aircrewmen who flew the Able Dog, and the troops who maintained it, are the real heroes of the Skyraider story. They are the ones who, confident in their skills and determined to get the job done in peace and war, went in harm's way. Their accounts, chronicled in this book, reflect the marvelous spirit of the American fighting man—his courage, his ingenuity, his humor, and his will to win. Together with the Skyraider they wrote a special chapter in the history of aviation and of the United States.

Ed Heinemann
Rancho Santa Fe, California
March 1982

Acknowledgments

I am indebted to many friends of the Skyraider without whose help this book could not have been written. In fact, by relating their Able Dog stories, a substantial number of these contributors wrote the book themselves. Ed Heinemann, the master himself, and Rear Admiral Henry Suerstedt, USN (Ret.), have been involved in the project from the outset, both in telling tales and in providing steadfast guidance and unwavering support. They were the flight leaders for the mission.

Beginning with a meeting in 1980 at Naval Air Station Miramar, California, deep in the heart of fighter pilot country, attack pilot Captain Paul Gray, USN (Ret.), has been aboard. His exploits in the Skyraider described in this volume were legendary long before the manuscript took form. Rear Admiral Ken Moranville, USN, a superlative leader and aviator, presented the relatively unknown account of his Skyraider days in Vietnam in 1960, when the war there itself was "unknown."

Captain Ed Greathouse, USN (Ret.), and Commander Charlie Hartman, USN, recounted their successful duel with North Vietnamese MiG-17s, as did a former naval lieutenant, Tom Patton. Greathouse also relived a story of the Spad on rescue combat air patrol duty. Commander Nick Daramus, USN, did likewise. Commander John Rochford, USN (Ret.), resurrected a 1954 episode in which Skyraiders downed a pair of Chinese Communist LA-7s. Rear Admiral Ken Knoizen, USN, passed on anecdotes from the Korean conflict to the Vietnam War and points in between. Captain Harry Ettinger, USN (Ret.), another veteran of those wars, described AD flying circa the late 1940s and afterward. Captain William L. Nyburg, USN (Ret.), remembered what those long low-levels were

Acknowledgments
like, and Jim Fausz, now director of the Champlin Fighter Museum in Mesa, Arizona, recalled his association with a favorite A-1E.

Many others were of immense help providing stories, information, photographs, and general support. These included: Admiral Thomas H. Moorer, USN (Ret.), former chairman of the Joint Chiefs of Staff and chief of naval operations who, despite a heavy schedule, always seems to find time to assist writers; Vice Admiral William I. Martin, a constant source of inspiration; Major John Elliott, USMC (Ret.), who provided essential data on Marine Corps Skyraiders; Vice Admiral Harold G. Bowen, USN (Ret.); Rear Admiral J. A. Thomas, USN (Ret.), who passed away early in 1982; Captain George Duncan, USN (Ret.); Captain Ted Wilbur, USNR (Ret.); Captain R. R. Worchesek, USN: Captain Paul Hollandsworth, USN; Captain Ralph Smith, USNR; Captain Jerry Canaan, USN (Ret.); Commander Al Nichols, USN; Commander Glenn W. Ward, USN (Ret.); Commander Art Syzmanski, USN (Ret.); Commander Cliff Ruthrauff, USN; and Commander Jim Reid, USN (Ret.).

Special salutes are in order for story tellers: Chief Warrant Officer (4) James W. Doran, USN; Aviation Boatswain's Mate Fueler John G. Gourley, USN; Richard F. Albright; L. Santos, Jr.; and J. C. Bowman.

Peter Mersky, an author, artist, and lieutenant commander in the U.S. Naval Reserve, not only produced the Skyraider line drawings but reviewed the manuscript. McDonnell-Douglas Corporation's Harry Gann, aviation historian, author, and accomplished aerial photographer, reviewed the narrative and supplied pictures. R. G. Smith, configuration engineer and artist, also of McDonnell-Douglas, looked over the text and contributed photographs of his paintings depicting the Skyraider in action. His capable assistant, Norma Bert, also checked the manuscript. Captain Matt Portz USNR (Ret.), director of information for The Aerospace Corporation, lent his expertise in reviewing the book before publication. I'm also beholden to professional editor Constance MacDonald for giving the manuscript a precision tune-up.

Others who assisted were Bob Canaday, formerly of McDonnell-Douglas, who helped with inputs from his long association with the AD; Barrett Tillman, prolific aviation author; Peter Kilduff, aviation buff and author; Bob Lawson, a great aerial photographer and editor of *The Hook*, the voice of the Tailhook Association, who presented photos and advice; Terry Treadwell, our British connection, who sent pictures of the Royal Navy's AEW.1 Skyraiders, with help from the Fleet Air Arm Museum; and Hal Andrews, an execu-

xiv

Skyraider

tive with Naval Air Systems Command and long-time contributing editor of *Naval Aviation News*, the official voice of U.S. naval aviation.

Captain Dick Knott, USN, head of Aviation Periodicals and History (including *Naval Aviation News*) and his staff, especially Helen Collins and Sandy Nye, pitched in without hesitation to assist. Thanks are particularly due to Clarke Van Vleet, naval aviation historian, who supplied some difficult and important details.

An extra measure of gratitude is due a gentleman already mentioned, Rear Admiral Hank Suerstedt, for his abiding support. Admiral Suerstedt personifies the consummate naval officer and aviator, and it is reassuring to know America produces leaders of his caliber. I wish I could have been his wingman.

I am also deeply beholden to my wife, Neta, and our children for always backing me up and for their marvelous endurance.

Abbreviations

AEW   airborne early warning

ASW   antisubmarine warfare

BuAer Bureau of Aeronautics

ECM   electronic countermeasures

LSO   landing signal officer

recce reconnaissance, usually used to define an armed recon-naissance flight

triple A anti-aircraft artillery

VA   an attack aircraft or squadron

VC   a composite squadron—consists of more than one type aircraft

VF   a fighter aircraft or squadron

SKYRAIDER

1

Start of a Saga

Nothing Must Interfere With The Completion Of This Airplane On Schedule.

> Inter-divisional Progress Report
> El Segundo Division of Douglas Aircraft
> Circa 1945

It was nearly 3 A.M. one June night in 1944, but the lights were still burning in a corner room on the seventh floor of the Statler Hotel in Washington, D.C. Inside that room, scattered about on end tables and the dresser were coffee cups, long since empty; remnants of sandwiches, long since consumed; and scraps of notepaper bearing endless columns of notes and numbers.

On a desk adjacent to the window, which looked out over the lamp-lit still life of a tranquil thoroughfare, were several poster-size sheets of paper, about two by five feet in dimension. Heavily outlined on the layered sheets were several views of an airplane, the most distinctive characteristic of which was its straightforward, uncomplicated design. Its unadorned style gave it an aura of simplicity and strength.

In shirtsleeves, their neckties loosened, the three weary men who had created the figures and the lines sat back in their chairs, exhausted. They had been laboring without intermission for nearly twelve hours. The tall, lean bespectacled leader of this triumvirate flipped a pencil onto the desk.

"That's it," said Ed Heinemann. "We'll have reproductions made on the way to the Main Navy building in the morning. For now, let's get a couple of hours sleep." Like the others, Heinemann was

Heinemann on wing chats with "Tailspin Tommy," LaVerne Brown, at El Segundo flight line in early Skyraider days. F3D Skyknight is in background.

4

Skyraider

drained of energy—an unusual condition for this thirty-six-year-old dynamo, who had risen to the summit as chief engineer of the El Segundo Division after only fifteen years with the California-based Douglas Aircraft Company. Twelve-hour working days were routine for him, and "late-night" efforts like this one, though uncommon, were part of the business in the competitive world of aircraft manufacturing. Yet despite the remarkable success of the SBD Dauntless, an El Segundo product that was credited with helping U.S. naval carrier pilots turn the tide of the war in the Pacific against the Japanese in 1942—and which was still carrying the fight to the enemy two years later—he was not a little worried for his company. Without a substantial contract, it was in for serious financial damage.

After Leo Devlin and Gene Root, Heinemann's top assistants, had left, the chief engineer lay back on his bed. Before drifting off to sleep he reviewed the key moments of the previous day, spent with officials at the Navy's Bureau of Aeronautics.

He had come east for a meeting about attack planes. The Navy badly needed a follow-on to the SBD Dauntless and the Curtiss SB2C Helldivers, aircraft that had been performing yeoman service in combat but were aging fast. Contracts had been let to the Martin Company, developing the XBTM (X represents "experimental") Mauler, and Henry Kaiser's Fleetwing organization, moving along with the XBTK. Douglas's entry, the BTD-1 Destroyer, successor to the short-lived SB2D, held some promise and had been ordered by the Navy but in limited number. The conference was to be a showdown of sorts between Douglas and the Navy. Although Fleetwing and Martin had met a week before to state their cases, it was apparent to Heinemann that a clear winner of the design competition had not yet been chosen. It was critical, however, that one be selected soon because the war was expected to continue for several more years. (Only a handful of people knew about the atomic bomb and the prospects that it might bring the Japanese to their knees and end the fighting.)

Experience gained in combat dictated new requirements for the attack aircraft that was to follow the Helldiver and Dauntless. Specifically, the Navy wanted a single-piloted aircraft that could carry bombs externally and that featured simple, maintainable systems. In addition, compared to existing planes, the attack/dive bomber, had to have:

—Shorter takeoff distance
—Increased combat radius

In addition to BTD-1 and SB2D, predecessors of the Skyraider included the success-ful SDD Dauntless.

—Increased rate of climb
—Greater load-carrying capability
—Greater stability and control

The meeting was held in the BuAer chief's conference room in the Main Navy building, a sprawling complex on Constitution Avenue situated between the Washington Monument and the Lincoln Memorial, and was chaired by assistant BuAer chief Rear Admiral Laurence B. Richardson. Captain Leslie C. Stevens, head of the research and development division was also present, along with Marine Corps Colonel Charles Fike, naval Captains Paul Ramsey and Walter Diehl, Commanders Tommy Thomas, Dave Shumway, and Emerson Fawkes, Lieutenant Commander John Ferguson, and

Skyraider

civilian expert Bill Frisbie. All were either aeronautical engineering specialists, aviators, or some combination of both.

The parley lasted most of the day. Discussion focused on whether or not the BTD was the answer to the Navy's needs. Would it be better than the Fleetwing or Martin entries?

Heinemann soon sensed that the military men had too many doubts about the BTD's potential. Driven as much by pride as the instinct to help his company survive, he quietly began to pursue a new line of thought.

Declarations about the BTD, pro and con, continued to fly across the conference table. Then, Heinemann made a decision that only he could make, fully realizing the risky path he was taking. At a break in the proceedings he asked for a moment or two to address the assembly. When the meeting reconvened, Heinemann was given the floor. He proceeded to make a statement as bold as it was disquieting.

"We would like to request that the Navy allow Douglas to cancel the existing contract for the BTD," he said, carefully measuring his words. There was an uneasy silence. He went on. "Instead, we ask permission to use the unexpended funds to build an entirely new bomber, one that I am convinced will do the job for you."

Whether or not the Navy's representatives, or even his own colleagues, believed that Heinemann had lost his marbles didn't matter at this point. What did matter was that a decisive step had been taken to resolve the pending controversy.

But there was a catch. Heinemann wanted a month—thirty days—to work up a new design proposal. The Navy didn't have the days to give, especially since Fleetwing and Martin were moving

XTB2D Skypirate.

along on a schedule; and it wasn't fair to the competition to dispense special consideration to Douglas.

Finally, Admiral Richardson agreed to the request. "But," he said, "you'll have to have a design for us by oh nine hundred tomorrow."

Ordinarily, it would be impossible to design an airplane complete with specifications in such a short time. But if he had doubts, Heinemann concealed them beneath a facade of self-assurance. Actually, in recent weeks he had been working unpretentiously on a single-seat, attack bomber design quite different from the BTD. It was planned with an R-2800 engine in mind, however, which was a drawback, since the Navy's specs called for a Wright R-3350 to power the attack bomber. This would present perplexing but solvable problems. (Martin was using the R-4360 engine, Fleetwing the R-2800. But the Navy had committed itself to purchasing R-3350s as well. Thus, Douglas had to plan on using them. Had the R-2800 been used, the Skyraider would have been a lighter aircraft.)

In spite of the uncertainties, this confrontation in a BuAer conference room became a turning point. It inspired Heinemann to change direction. It was time to move the design that had been simmering on a back burner to the front of the stove with the flame full up.

Before rushing back to the Statler, Heinemann telephoned Douglas Vice President Art Raymond and cleared the idea with him. He next called Donald Douglas himself, also at the corporate offices in Santa Monica, and explained his actions. The legendary designer and founder of the company that bore his name believed in his protege, listened thoughtfully, asked a few questions, then endorsed the plan. In this hour, never far from conscious thought, were the words Donald Douglas had spoken to Heinemann many years before:

"Navy planes take a beating. They slam down on the carriers when they land and get roughed up by the unforgiving elements of the high seas. If we want the Navy to buy our planes we must build them rugged. They have to take punishment and still work."

The man from El Segundo had to be sure that above all, this attack bomber would be rugged and able to take punishment. With the image of a spanking new dive bomber swimming briefly through his mind, he fell asleep.

Early the next morning he, Devlin, and Root found a blueprint shop, had copies of their work reproduced, and taxied back to the Main Navy building. By nine o'clock, Heinemann had unveiled the drawings, specifications, and predicted performance figures to several of the key participants in the previous day's heated session. The three men waited impatiently and not without a measure of consternation as the documents were routed quickly through a series of cognizant offices.

Finally, before noon, word was undramatically passed to Heinemann that "Yes, it was OK for the remaining BTD funds to be used for a redesign effort." But it was stipulated that the first article, or aircraft, had to fly in nine months.

The Navy's decision was less a sanction of the new concept than an agreement to allow more time for Douglas, hopefully, to come up with a winner. Still, one or more knowledgeable individuals in the naval hierarchy must have detected the intrinsically sound nature of this fresh concept. Some must have sensed that here, quite possibly, was a rugged enough machine, one able to take punishment and, most important, capable of contributing to victory.

The El Segundo men were elated. They were no longer on the ropes but were still in the ring with a few more rounds to fight. They flew back to California buoyed with hope and anxious to slug away at the invigorating challenge that lay ahead.

So it is that many believe the Skyraider was designed overnight in a hotel room in the nation's capital. Not exactly true. But no matter. What Ed Heinemann and his partners accomplished that marathon evening is the stuff of legend, perhaps. It is the intensity of their skilled efforts in an abbreviated period of time, however, that should be celebrated. It was their ability to work and create under immense pressure that dramatized the achievement. Had Heinemann, Devlin, and Root failed, the Douglas company would have suffered inestimable economic loss. What they really did was to modify and fine-tune in a fantastic hurry a basic attack bomber design that was already in the making through an evolutionary process manifested by the SBD, SB2D, BTD, and even older flying machines. The Able Dog, like a fine and enduring sculpture, was the final image left standing after the chipping and smoothing away of unnecessary edges was done.

Back at El Segundo all hands swung into action. Heinemann was not at all reluctant to give pep talks, and shortly after reaching his office he summoned his staffers. He briefly outlined the objective, emphasizing the first-flight deadline nine months hence. He explained that the new plane must feature more lift but less weight. It had to weigh 16,500 pounds compared to the BTD's 18,000. The

A2D Skyshark.

maximum lift coefficient, a measure of the aircraft's aerodynamic efficiency, had to be increased from a factor of 1.8 to 2.0. Importantly, fueling, arming, and maintenance time had to be reduced by 50 percent. By early July, the engineering staff was fully immersed in the project.

Reid Bogert was the project engineer but suffered a case of viral encephalitis and was replaced by Leonard Quick. Tooling was under way by August. The plane even had a new name. It was to be called the BT2D Dauntless II in deference to its predecessor, the SBD Dauntless I.

Among other central figures involved in the project was R. G. Smith, a configuration engineer who ultimately gained international acclaim for his aviation paintings. He was instrumental to the BT2D and many other aircraft. R. G. had a unique ability to grasp a design concept and convert ideas to specific lines and curves on paper. Heinemann relied on him regularly. Exceptionally patient and persevering, Smith was able to respond rapidly to changes, drawing and redrawing the aircraft, sections of it, and the multitude of components that were integral to it.

Meanwhile, BuAer agreed to most of the ongoing alterations inherent in the developing stages of an aircraft. Progress was rapid. A special bulletin was published at the plant in November of 1944. It was an informal document but one designed to inform and inspire the war workers.

"The BT2D will be underweight," declared the opening sentence. The paper went on to detail weight reduction goals. A careful analysis indicated the BT2D could be built with a final weight of 1,147

pounds below the guarantee. In deference to possible overconfi-
dence or error, the underweight goal was established as 1,000
pounds.

"If 1,000 pounds are saved," said the bulletin, "the BT2D will be
able to double its normal bomb load and still meet specified performance. Or, it will be able to carry a 1,000 pound bomb for a
combat radius of 610 nautical miles with the same takeoff distance
that current fighter-bombers use in combat when carrying a 150-
gallon drop tank and a 500-pound bomb."

Specifics aside, the point was that this attack plane could be
better than any of its predecessors. Among the ingredients for success were Heinemann's disciplined leadership, his believing and
skilled design staff, and a manpower force of men and women who
wanted to give their fighting men the best possible weapons to
eradicate the enemy. An almost palpable "must-do" spirit perme-
ated the Douglas facility and its people.

The concentration on saving weight paid off. In the months that
followed, unnecessary poundage was eliminated. Final weight was
less than what Douglas guaranteed the Navy. In addition to satis-
fying the overall improved performance demands imposed by the
Navy, the BT2D featured:

—A simplified fuel system with a single, internal tank.
—Dive brakes on the fuselage (instead of on the wings), which
   permitted seventy-degree dive-bombing angles. (Even with the
   emphasis on weight saving, the BT2D, like other new aircraft,
   was inevitably heavier and denser than its predecessors. In
   vertical—90 degree—dives it would exceed safe pull-out
   speeds. The SBD, for instance, dove vertically at 250 knots. The
   BT2D could not be held to that speed. Therefore dive angles for
   it were reduced to a maximum of 70 degrees.)
—Elimination of a bomb bay with, instead, wing racks and
   mounting points installed that enabled bombs, rockets, and
   extra fuel tanks to be carried externally.
—An electrically actuated "explosive charge" bomb rack release
   system whereby stores were "pushed" away from the aircraft
   into the airstream.
—A pair (later four) of twenty-millimeter cannons mounted inside either wing.
—300-knot diving speed.
—A roomy cockpit devoid of fuel, oil, or hydraulic "plumbing"
   routed through it.

—Easy-to-read cockpit instruments. (This was part of a major human engineering effort. For example, studies showed that the pilot's eyes were normally about twenty-four inches from the gages; so the numbers on the instruments were modified in size for comfortable and instant reading. Also, although not the case on the initial models, the gear, flap, and dive brake controls were designed to look like the actual items they controlled. Further, to extend the flaps, the handle was pushed down, in the *same direction* as the flaps actually moved. The same was true for the landing wheels and dive brakes.)

—Folding wings to accommodate parking evolutions on the crowded carriers.

—An electrically controlled, hydraulically boosted horizontal stabilizer.

There were many other improvements. But the predominant characteristic of the BT2D throughout was the sturdy, clean-lined simplicity of its design.

Meanwhile, Kaiser Fleetwing's XBTK ran into some difficulties and was unable to make scheduled test flights in October 1944. These were reset for March 1945. Martin's XBTM, on the other hand, completed initial flights at the Navy's Patuxent River, Maryland test base. It was slightly overweight and needed some modifications, however. Consequently, Douglas-El Segundo had closed the time gap. As one headline on an interdivisional progress reported urged: "Nothing Must Interfere with the Completion of This Airplane on Schedule." Nothing did.

Two weeks ahead of schedule, on 18 March 1945, at Mines airfield [now the site of Los Angeles International Airport] adjacent to the El Segundo plant, the first of what would eventually number 3,180 Able Dogs was ready to leave the ground. A colorful and competent test pilot named LaVerne Brown (also known as "Tailspin Tommy" for his role in flying adventure movies of the day) trooped out to the flight line, stepped up onto the wing, inserted himself in the cockpit, and strapped in.

With a small but anxious gathering watching, he cranked over the enormous propeller, the arc of which peaked sixteen feet above the concrete. First black, then pure white clouds of smoke shot out from exhaust manifolds on either side of the nose. These were accompanied by the powerful rumble of the eighteen-cylinder Wright R-3350 engine chugging into action. The smoke disappeared quickly as the engine settled down to a smooth idle.

AD-1 with rockets on racks. Note single, 20-millimeter cannon on wing. Later versions had two on either side.

Brown made some preliminary checks then signaled ground crewmen to remove the chocks. He began to slowly taxi the first article, BT2D Bureau Number 09085. It was ready for its maiden excursion into the blue.

Several minutes later, aligned on the runway, Brown advanced the throttle full forward. The R-3350 responded mightily, and the attack bomber bellowed down the strip into the prevailing wind. Approaching fifty knots the tail smoothly came up so that the fuselage was parallel to the runway. Seconds later the Dauntless II rose from the field, seemingly without effort. It was as if the machine had a life of its own and knew that is belonged aloft, up and away from the earth.

That was the beginning of an exceptionally successful test flight. Brown put the bird through basic maneuvers, and after about an hour airborne returned and landed. The aircraft settled comfortably onto the runway and rolled to an uneventful stop.

A short time later back at the starting point, Brown descended from the stilled machine. He was no sooner on the ground patting the fuselage proudly than he began extolling the aircraft's virtues.

The BT2D, he stated, gave every indication that it was the plane that everybody thought it could be.

Other tests with additional Dauntless IIs continued, and in early April the Navy began more advanced examinations at Patuxent River. The aircraft received above-average grades, exceeding expectations for the most part. In May the Navy ordered 548 of the attack bombers. Problems and setbacks did occur, but they were usually ironed out without major difficulty. Everyone at the El Segundo plant and naval personnel close to the project agreed that the BT2D was a winner.

Because the war ended in 1945, the BT2D did not experience combat as expected. In fact, the original order for airplanes was reduced, reflecting decreased U.S. defense needs. So, while there was jubilation that the conflict was over, there was also disappointment in some quarters because of an inevitable slowing down of aircraft manufacturing. No one could know then, of course, that the attack bomber would have ample opportunity to test its merit in the crucible of combat. In a few years the orders for the Dauntless II would multiply.

In February 1946, the Navy's designation system was altered. Douglas Aircraft was assigned the "Sky-" series of nomenclature. The Dauntless II thus became the A (for Attack) D (for Douglas) Skyraider. (The term Able Dog was derived from the phonetic alphabet used by the military in earlier years—A for Able, B for Baker, C for Charlie, D for Dog, and so on. During the Vietnam war, when the supposedly aging Skyraider continued to share the skies with jets, it was nicknamed the "Spad" in friendly reference to a World War I combat plane.)

Fleetwing's entry into the competition never reached fruition. Martin's BTM became the AM-1 Mauler, 180 of which were ordered.

By Christmastime 1946 fleet squadrons and Marine Corps units began receiving their AD-1s. Attack Squadron Nineteen A, home-based at Naval Air Station Alameda, in the San Francisco area, was the first outfit to get the aircraft. The Skyraider era was soon in full flower.

By 1949 the Navy had taken delivery of its 500th Skyraider, each one costing a very reasonable 250,000 to 285,000 dollars. In only four years there had been no fewer than twenty-two versions of Heinemann's basic design, some short-lived and experimental in nature but all reflecting the requirements of strategic planners. These versions represented modifications of four basic types: the

Skyraider

AD-1, AD-2, AD-3, and AD-4. They demonstrated the Skyraider's flexibility and adaptability. They clearly showed that the AD could handle various missions such as night attack, antisubmarine warfare, radar countermeasures, target towing, and utility/transport—in addition to its principal assignment: daytime attack.

Only one modification of the initial model, the AD-1, appeared (although experimentation with various mission equipment, such as airborne early warning gear, took place). It was the AD-1Q, configured with radar for countermeasures assignments. The -1, incidentally, experienced structural problems during carrier landings that led to a strengthening of the wing and tail sections.

The AD-2's power plant was beefed up, giving the R-3350 an additional 200 horsepower. It was in this model that the cockpit controls were designed to resemble the systems they actuated. The dive brake control, for instance, looked like a miniature dive brake instead of a knob. Like its predecessor, the AD-2 had only one different version, the AD-2Q for radar countermeasures, called RCM in those days.

With the arrival of the AD-3, the Skyraider's basic design proved itself genuinely adaptable to multiple versions and, therefore, multiple missions. Included were the countermeasure -3Q; the -3N for night attack; the -3W for airborne early warning; the -3E for early warning and ASW search; and the -3S for night and ASW attack.

A tow target version, -U, was also used. A "package" attached to its centerline bomb rack housed a reel that could stream out a cable two miles long. Apart from the pure attack version, this and the other "multi-mission" types accommodated one or more crewmen in the fuselage. In the case of the target-towing Skyraider, a crewman connected yellow cloth sleeves to the end of the cable through a door in the bottom of the fuselage. Swept aft by the airstream as the pilot let out the reel, the sleeves made excellent targets for fighter aircraft to practice their air-to-air marksmanship. The reel was retracted hydraulically. In case of trouble—entanglement in an aircraft, for instance—an explosive charge drove a guillotine fitting that automatically severed the cable.

The AD-3 featured an Aeroproducts propeller, better than earlier types, lengthened landing gear oleo struts, stronger landing gear, and strengthened wing structure for work aboard the carrier. It also had a reinforced fuselage, a new tail wheel, an air bottle for emergency blow-back of the canopy, and some other cockpit refinements.

In the AD-4 category there were the -Q, -N, and -W versions.

Better radar was now available—the APS-19A replaced the previously used APS-4. The P-1 autopilot was added to relieve the pilot on long-range or long endurance missions.

In the -N version, the rear "cockpit" housed a radar navigator and a countermeasures operator, normally enlisted specialists. The -Q carried a radar countermeasures operator. Some -Qs could be modified for -U, or utility missions, such as target towing, and carried an additional man to handle towing chores. The -W accommodated two radar operators in addition to the pilot.

Interestingly, the Skyraider was the first single-engine aircraft to carry a special (atomic) weapon. Ed Heinemann's group was tasked with designing the installation requirements, and R. G. Smith made numerous drawings depicting the entire modification early in 1951 and after. Flights with the simulated weapon were made in the same year. An AD-4—Bureau Number 123805—was the aircraft involved. Strict security was, of course, in effect at the time, and the project was very hush-hush.

Despite the seeming complexity of the letter designations, the various missions, the diversity of the aircraft, and the broad range of equipment that was adapted to it, the AD was still easier to maintain than its predecessors—an important consideration in its use.

AD-3W with "Guppy" radar pod and external fuel tank.

16

Skyraider

In the late 1940s the military services underwent serious cuts in strength, an expected consequence of the long war. Harry Ettinger was a young aviator then, destined to fly Skyraiders in two wars in the years to come. He was in attack Squadron 55 in 1949, and remembered those austere days. In the fall of that year the squadron received spanking new AD-4s that replaced the AD-1s they were issued a few months earlier. Before that his unit had operated TBM Avengers.

Ettinger, who flew virtually all of the Skyraider models in his career, took a special liking to the -4. "It had a unique feature compared to all other ADs," said Ettinger, "and that was its ability to reach high altitudes."

Because of across-the-board reductions in funding, bravo (flight) funds were in short supply. Said Ettinger, "Someone got the idea that VF-52 which was a jet transition squadron in our CAG (Carrier Air Group Five) flying TO-1 Shooting Star jets, could lend our squadron some funds for the mutual benefit of both. Part of VF-52's syllabus called for instrument work and because the AD-4 could operate at altitude with the TO-1s, VA-55 aviators could chase (monitor) the jet pilots as they concentrated on their cockpit gages practicing instrument flight. The fighter squadron wouldn't have to send up another gas-guzzling jet to accompany the first and the Skyraider pilots would gain precious flight time."

On a typical jet-with-prop flight the two planes would rendezvous at 20,000 feet over the San Diego Radio range and fly at an indicated airspeed of 200 knots. The Shooting Star pilot went "under the bag," on the gages, and did his thing as the Skyraider followed, ensuring the way was clear and advising the pilot as necessary.

Some time later Ettinger and his fellow pilots were engaged in a more dramatic exhibition of the AD-4's high-flying ability. There was a serious, ongoing battle for funds between the Navy and the Air Force, the latter service opting for an increased strategic bomber force among other things. Of course, the Navy thought that money was better spent by purchasing modern aircraft and aircraft carriers.

B-36s were setting distance records for the Air Force, making nonstop flights of great distances without refueling. One of their preplanned missions featured a route that extended from Carswell in Texas to Seattle, on to Hawaii, then back to Southern California, and, ultimately, to Texas again. An AirPac (Commander Naval Air Forces Pacific) staffer wanted the Navy to show up the super bomb-

This Naval Air Test Center AD-2, pictured in 1950, carries a torpedo, two World War II-vintage 500 pounders, and a full load of five-inch HVARs.

Skyraider without wheel fairings has dive brakes extended and is carrying large Tiny Tim rockets plus a dozen high velocity aircraft rockets (HVARs).

18

Skyraider

ers. The plan was for prop-driven ADs to intercept the B-36s as a sort of professional slap in the face. VA-55 was assigned the mission.

As the lumbering bombers proceeded on the inbound leg from Hawaii, AirPac alerted its P2V Neptune patrol planes, operating 500 miles offshore, to try to detect them. Radar-equipped ADs or TBM Guppies concentrated on the area 200 miles off the coast. When the B-36s reached this area, VA-55 AD-4s were launched.

Said Ettinger, "We'd take off from North Island on an assigned heading and contact the Guppy for vector information, all the while climbing to 36,000 feet which took a long 18 to 20 minutes. From that height the B-36s, which were at 32,000 to 34,000 feet, were easy to spot. We would make one or two high side runs, filming the action with gun cameras. Those one or two runs were about all the AD could hack that high above the ground but we made a point."

For what they were worth, the films were sent to AirPac to prove that naval props could match skills with the best of the strategic bombers.

One phase of "mixed-bag" air group training included tactics similar to "Alpha Strikes," which were massive assaults flown against North Vietnamese targets a quarter century later. Ettinger's AD-4s, carrying a single bomb apiece for practice purposes, were the base element in the multi-plane formation gathered at 36,000 feet. A group of F9F Panthers were above them loaded with 100 rounds of ammo, while a squadron of F4U Corsairs, each with two HVARs (five-inch, Zuni, high velocity aircraft rockets), were in trail slightly below the jets. A second squadron of Panthers was at 32,000 feet.

The plan was to approach the simulated target, Castle Rock, located on San Clemente Island off the California coast, head-on. Said Ettinger, "When the flight leader signalled the attack to begin, the lower F9Fs rolled in at a shallow 20-degree angle to strafe the target area, softening up the enemy and suppressing AAA (antiaircraft artillery) emplacements. The Corsairs then dove in with rockets using a 50-degree dives. Our ADs, speed brakes extended, banked in steeply on 70-degree dive angles. The remaining Panthers swept in for a final strafing pass, assuming there was no threat from opposing fighters. The whole maneuver was quite an adventure.

"If the timing was right the Skyraiders would be releasing their bombs as the last of the Corsairs was coming off the target and the Panthers were arriving to strafe. Having come from TBMs, it was most stimulating to operate way up there with the jet set. Adjusting

wasn't easy though. For one thing, we weren't used to oxygen masks
and kept ours stowed until climbing through 12,000 feet. We didn't
want those nose bags on until absolutely necessary.

"On the roll-in from 36,000 it was mandatory to actuate the
brakes right away," Ettinger recalled. "We would gather speed so
quickly at that altitude that it was possible to exceed the design
airspeed limits at which the brakes could actually open. The
'boards' slowed the plane tremendously, and the target seemed an
eternity away. We trimmed up for the long trip down, stabilizing at
about 285 knots. Descending through 20,000 feet we took off the
mask and stowed it in the receptacle provided. It took ages but
when we reached 10,000 feet we began serious concentration on the
target. We usually released the bomb at 2,000 feet, bottoming out in
the dive at 1,000. While the tactic was reasonably successful, we
never employed it in Korea. We were more effective operating
closer to the ground over there." (Ettinger was transferred to VC-35
and trained in night attack work before going into combat in 1951.)

When North Korean Communist forces crossed the 38th parallel
to invade South Korea on 25 June 1950, six years from the concep-

This AD-4 set a load-carrying record at NAS Dallas, Texas, in May 1953 when it was
flown with 10,500 pounds of bombs on board, 3,000 pounds more than its basic
weight.

AD-4 undergoes catapult test at Lakehurst, N.J.

tion of the Skyraider, the attack bomber was in its fourth series of development. There was much more to learn about the airplane, but it had already excited the world of naval aviation with its accomplishments.

In any event, it was Attack Squadron 55, operating aboard the Seventh Fleet carrier USS *Valley Forge*, that took the attack bomber into combat action for the first time.

The fleet had been placed on alert shortly after the outbreak of hostilities in Korea. But it wasn't until eight days later, after the *Valley Forge* sortied in a hurry from Hong Kong, that a wave of piston planes, Chance-Vought F4U Corsairs and a dozen Skyraiders led by VA-55's Lieutenant Commander N. D. Hodson, struck Pyongyang airfield and associated installations. Jets from the carrier, seeing combat for the first time in the U.S. Navy, also joined the attack following a massive, early-morning launch from the flattop. It was 3 July, the eve of America's Independence Day.

The most realistic Hollywood combat film, even in 3-D with wraparound stereophonic sound, could not convey the menacing rumble of Hodson's Skyraiders during the attack.

The dark-blue-colored AD-4s carried a pair of 500 pounders and six 100 pounders each. They plowed through cloudy weather over the sea, but from their roll-in altitude of 7,000 feet found the airfield under clear skies.

Ear-crackling explosions ripped skyward as the Americans dove, released their bombs, and roared up and away for repeat runs, destroying or damaging aircraft, hangars, and barracks buildings. Storage facilities were left ablaze. Secondary fires blossomed from ammunition dumps. A fuel storage farm received a direct hit. Bomb craters pock-marked the runway. Jets and props shared the credit.

The raid was a success, and on the Fourth of July, twenty-four hours later, Hodson's flyers celebrated by knocking out a bridge span and destroying ten locomotives. In a portent of the way the Skyraider mission in Korea was to be characterized, four VA-55 birds took hits from ground fire. The U.S. Navy and its air arm, however, had served notice it was a power to be reckoned with.

On the other hand, communist forces were to demonstrate a tenacity that would ultimately prove equal to that put forth by United Nations units. In any event, the Skyraider was in its element, the war was on, and it would be a long time before the Land of Morning Calm was tranquil again.

Interdiction

What is he trying to do? Bust 'em up faster than I can fix 'em?

> Lieutenant (Junior Grade) Andrew "Ski"
> Syzmanski, VF-54 maintenance officer, in
> reference to his skipper, Commander
> Paul Gray

Some called it a war fought to prevent a larger war. When it was over, few believed there was a clear victory by either the Communists or the United Nations forces. Opinions and history aside, the fighting that raged for more than three years on the Korean peninsula provided the AD Skyraider its baptism under fire. In the capable hands of those who piloted it, the aircraft responded in splendid fashion, proving it could satisfy the requirements and demands placed on it.

Bounded by Russia to the northeast and China to the north, Korea was no stranger to conflict and the ravages of battle. Though Chinese culture flourished there through much of the period after Christ, it was invaded by Mongols in the thirteenth century, and the Japanese 300 years later. The Land of the Rising Sun recognized Korea's independence in 1148, but the Chinese still looked upon Korea as their vassal. This led to Korea's uniting with Japan in the Sino-Japanese War of 1894–1895. The Russo-Japanese War ten years later resulted from the desire of these two countries to gain influence in Korea.

Korea was annexed by the Japanese in 1910 but was ultimately freed of Japanese control after World War II. By 1948 the 38th parallel had become a dividing line separating two zones of occupa-

North Korean road and railway center comes under attack by steep-diving ADs.

tion: Russia to the north, the United States to the south. North Korea thus became the communist Democratic People's Republic of Korea while South Korea became the Republic of Korea.

The terrain of this peninsula which juts southward from the eastern flank of the Asian continent with the Yellow Sea to the west, the Sea of Japan to the east, is mountainous, especially in the north where peaks reach more than 8,000 feet skyward. Winters are brutal, as many American soldiers and airmen discovered in the fighting.

By October 1950, three carriers were on station with Task Force 77 off the eastern coast of Korea: the Happy Valley (*Valley Forge*), the Phil Sea, (USS *Philippine Sea*), and the USS *Leyte*. In November the Chinese entered the war, and the American units were assigned to strangle supply lines, specifically the half dozen major bridges that straddled the Yalu River, which formed much of the border between Korea and Manchuria. (Naval air was to handle operations over Northeast Korea, while the U.S. Air Force was responsible for the western part.) Armed reconaissance missions wherein aircraft searched for and destroyed targets of opportunity were also prevalent. This was interdiction in the truest sense of the word, which by military definition means "to prevent or hinder by any means, enemy use of an area or route." Interdiction then, could be called the code word of the Korean War as far as naval aviation was concerned, and no airplane could interdict better than the Skyraider.

For nearly two years interdiction was a principal occupation of the Task Force 77 naval units. Close air support of ground forces, another mission for which the AD was gifted, was also a major responsibility.

Both were arduous undertakings. For one thing there was an enormous area to cover with a comparatively small number of carrier-based aircraft, roughly 150 planes. In a frustrating parallel to the scenario that would face American and Allied forces in Vietnam years later, the Communists proved extremely adept in supplying forces in the South despite resistance. Using 8,000 or so trucks, hundreds of trains, proliferating antiaircraft artillery, an expertise in camouflaging their rolling stock, and, as often as necessary, the cloak of night to move food, fuel, and arms, they tested the very capacity of naval aviation to wage combat.

Exacerbating their already difficult task, the U.S. flyers were ordered not to violate Chinese airspace, an especially maddening

VA-115 AD-4 loaded with HVARs is directed into position aboard the USS *Philippine Sea* for launch against Korean targets, September 1950.

restriction since the Yalu was a border in itself, and obviously the bridges connected the two countries.

A typical strike group from each carrier consisted of a mix of Skyraiders, Corsairs, and F9F Panthers, numbering between 24 and 40 aircraft depending on the mission. The ADs routinely carried a pair of 1,000 pounders and an occasional 2,000-pound bomb, plus full buckets of ammunition.

In the first six months of 1951 the focus of action was on the eastern coastal network of roads and railways between Wonsan and Chongjun. The Korean winter in those early months of the year was at its worst, with snow, sleet, ice, and always the cold. Hundreds of miles of railroad tracks, nearly a thousand bridges and causeways, and more than 200 tunnels were identified as targets. The predominantly mountainous terrain accounted for the proliferation of tunnels.

While stories abound concerning the attacks on the bridges in those months, the assaults on one near Kilchu were particularly dramatic. A key bridge connecting two tunnels across a 600-foot-wide ravine, it was of immense strategic and logistic importance to the North Koreans. A majority of supplies moving south from Man-

Skyraider

churia along the northeast rail system had to cross this concrete and steel affair.

Even after repeated attacks, the enemy managed to make the bridge usable by reinforcing it with wooden beams. So, naval pilots hit it with napalm, which burned the wood. But two of the six spans remained. Mission followed mission as the Reds, often working through the dark of night, put the bridge back into operating condition.

It took 2,000-pound bombs to immobilize the structure. The commanding officer of VA-195 on board the USS *Princeton*, Harold G. "Swede" Carlson, was credited with leading the strikes that dropped the major spans of the bridge. He and his squadron mates flew AD-4 Skyraiders. The bridge spanned what thus came to be known as "Carlson's Canyon," in honor of the skipper.

Still, what was particularly frustrating to the flyers was the ability of the enemy to repair, overnight, bridges for which pilots had just braved a hail of fire, in knocking them out the previous day. (Vietnam-era aircrews would share the same frustrations.)

The Communists also were masters at camouflage. For example,

VA-35 Skyraider makes a deck run aboard the USS *Leyte* in combat zone, November 1950.

wooden platforms were rigged atop Soviet-built tanks to make them look like trucks. A variety of other devices made life harder for the pilots.

Ensign Louis C. Page, flying a Skyraider from the *Philippine Sea* early in the war, was looking over a railroad yard and noted a haystack incongruously positioned near the tracks.

"It was a beautiful stack, the most natural one I'd ever seen," he said. "But haystacks and railroad yards just don't go together."

He armed his cannons, rolled in, and sprayed 20 mike mike (millimeter) into the stack. It exploded into an orange-black cloud, indicating that the hay was concealing either fuel drums or weapons or some combination of both.

To appreciate one Korean War pilot, let's jump ahead for a moment to another war in the Far East. It's the late 1960s.

A helicopter rumbled over the battle-scarred underbrush of South Vietnam's delta region. Suddenly, there was the crackle of ground fire. Bullets stitched their way through the hull of the Huey gunship, spraying shrapnel throughout the whirlybird's interior. Some small, jagged fragments ripped into the flesh of naval Captain Paul Gray, who was riding in the helo in his capacity as commander of the U.S. Navy's Riverine Patrol Forces. Gray winced in pain but knew instinctively that his wounds were not terribly serious. Yet he had to wonder in those perilous moments as the helicopter vibrated noisily, struggling to stay aloft, if the odds were finally catching up with him.

After he had fought in three wars and held positions of command in each of them, was the grim reaper's scythe swinging toward him now, on this humid afternoon in the skies of Southeast Asia?

Fortunately, no. Gray and the helicopter crew survived and the captain was able to continue his duties. He completed the combat tour and retired from the Navy in 1969 after an almost unbelievable career, one that carried him from the Naval Academy, class of 1941, through battleship duty, flight training, thirty combat missions in the Pacific in World War II, and beyond. In that global war, he served as executive and commanding officer of a torpedo and a dive bombing squadron, respectively, piloting the Curtiss SB2C Helldiver. In the Korean War he was skipper of VF-54 (an attack squadron despite the "F," for fighter, designation), where he flew AD-3 and AD-4 Skyraiders on 120 combat sorties. Finally, after various assignments between wars, including command of the USS *Kearsarge*, an aircraft carrier, he skippered the Riverine Patrol Forces in Vietnam, known in the vernacular as the "Brown Water Navy." All told, he had a dozen commands and at one point had earned more combat decorations then any other officer in the U.S. Navy.

The irony of a career during which he was exposed with considerable regularity to enemy guns is that he weathered the first two conflicts as a pilot unscathed, only to be wounded twice in Vietnam—once in the helo and on another occasion in the jungle when he caught shrapnel again, this time from a land mine that had been actuated by a trip wire.

Even more remarkable is the fact that Paul Gray, one of the most tenacious and aggressive aviators to pin on the Gold Wings, was shot down or forced to ditch, or emergency land, *five times* in Korea. He survived each episode—two on land, three in the icy seas of Wonson Harbor—despite a law of averages that surely dictated that Paul Gray should not leave Korea alive.

Gray and the Skyraider went together like Patton and tanks. Like the attack bomber, this pilot was durable and could take punishment. He took the reigns of VF-54, based aboard the carrier USS *Essex*, in 1951. Before long he was leading attacks on targets of opportunity with great effect. His method: go in low and press for accuracy. The targets were bridges, railroad tracks, railroad cars, trucks, troop emplacements, and supply depots. Forward air controllers (FACs) on the ground or in U.S. Air Force spotter planes aloft often coordinated attacks, vectoring the bombers toward the targets. Most missions took place during the day. Sorties were often an arduous, butt-busting four and a half hours in length. Casualty rates were high. Gray's squadron, for instance, suffered 25 percent losses on the cruise, which lasted twelve months in 1951–1952. Seven pilots were killed.

A native of St. John, Kansas, Gray was a thirty-five-year-old in Korea, who kept in shape with workouts in the ship's gym. This helped to sustain him on the long combat fights and certainly didn't work against him when he had to crash-land his ADs.

"We seldom got over 1,000 feet above the ground," said Gray, "and frequently returned to the ship with holes in the Skyraider's skin from small arms fire. But the AD was a marvelous machine and could carry the same tonnage in bombs as the four-engine B-17 bomber of just a few years earlier. [A couple of years later at Naval Air Station Dallas, Texas, an AD took off with load of fuel and ordnance totaling 26,739 pounds, an amount equal to a DC-3 transport carrying 24 passengers.] It was a perfect aircraft for close air support and the other bombing and strafing duty which characterized the interdiction mission."

Another Korean Skyraider pilot put it this way: "An altimeter reading didn't mean a thing (flying an AD) in Korea. We were going up a hill or coming down one. Providing you could see the end of it in time, you could fly down inside a dead end canyon in an Able Dog and still get out of it. In fact, the Reds finally started stringing cables across canyons to keep us out!"

Close air support, Korea style, was basically the same as that practiced by naval and Marine Corps flyers and ground units in World War II and even before. Spotters on the ground at the front radioed target positions to the attack aircraft above. Joint communications were the key. For the ADs, a typical close air support mission load included 400 rounds of twenty-millimeter ammunition, three 500 pounders, and a dozen five-inch rockets. Because the Skyraider could linger on station and its overall endurance was about four hours, it was obvious that the Douglas attack plane was perfectly suited for such missions.

According to one story, a ground operator asked the leader of a newly arrived flight of ADs assigned to support Allied troops, "What ordnance are you carrying?" The pilot, laden with a full assortment of weaponry, replied, "You name it, we got it!"

Demonstrating a mild disdain for the "call-sign" system with which pilots identified themselves by an officially designated name followed by a three-digit side number, Gray's group decided on a Walt Disney theme. Gray became Snow White and his wingmen Dopey, Grumpy, Sneezy, and so forth. It was not long after he implemented this system that Gray's Skyraider took a hit while over enemy territory.

"Happily for me," said Gray, "shortly after I went into the sea a South Korean picket boat came along and pulled me to safety."

There was more to it than that. Gray's Skyraider sank quickly beneath him after he splashed into the water. Somehow he unlatched himself from the cockpit, but, as he put it, "I was weighted down by my survival equipment which included pistol, ammunition belt, Mae West, and various other items. I couldn't quickly locate the CO_2 cartridge toggles of the Mae West, even though they were floating somewhere directly in front of me. I started to sink but got to the toggles in time and the South Koreans then hauled me out of the water."

On board the carrier the crew received the good news from Grumpy, Gray's wingman orbiting overhead. "Snow White is safe!" he reported with a sharp ring of exuberance in his voice.

Skyraider

Wonsan Harbor, where Gray ditched, incidentally, is a major seaport on Korea's east coast. Shielded from storms by a natural barrier of mountains, it is ice-free in winter. It was, therefore, a reasonably accommodating place to ditch an airplane as long as survivors weren't left in the frigid waters too long in the non-summer seasons.

Gray's philosophy of go-in-low-for-accuracy had its drawbacks. When a bomb released from a fast-moving aircraft explodes, it inevitably sends a pattern of fragments skyward. The pilot has only fractions of a second to pull up and away if he releases at low altitude, where he stands a chance of sustaining hits from his own weapon.

VA-195 AD is loaded with a 1,000 pounder and 6.5-inch anti-tank aircraft rockets (ATARs), which could penetrate 18 inches of armor plate. ATAR was reputed to be the only rocket at the time that could stop the Soviet-built T-36 tank.

Several days after his first dip in Korean waters, Gray angled his Skyraider toward the mouth of a tunnel in which the enemy had stowed a locomotive. He pickled off (released) a 1,000 pounder and banked swiftly away. The bomb apparently struck just at the mouth of the tunnel, a good hit. Fragments from it slammed into his AD, however, producing ominous thudding sounds. The plane was barely flyable, and since making it to the ship was in doubt, Gray advised his wingmen that he would try to reach an emergency landing strip called K-55. Somehow he managed to coax the wounded plane southward across the 38th parallel to the field, where he landed.

On the ground at K-55, mechanics examined the bird, shook their heads, and declared it "dead." It was scrapped, and Gray was flown out to the *Essex*. Within twenty-four hours he was aloft in another Skyraider over North Korea on a combat mission.

A few days later Gray swept in low over a target, collected no less than fifty-nine holes in the skin of his attack bomber from ground fire, told the carrier that he thought he could recover on board, and proceeded to do so with minimum dramatics. It was almost like another day at the office for Paul Gray.

Fortunately, this plane could be repaired although the sight of those holes angered one Andrew Syzmanski, a lieutenant (junior grade) and VF-54 maintenance officer tasked with patching up the aircraft on board the *Essex*. A native of Brooklyn known as much for his salty language as his great repair skills, "Ski" could only ask the rhetorical question, "What is he trying to do? Bust 'em up faster than I can fix 'em?"

Some time later as Gray was engaged in an attack on a column of North Korean trucks, an enemy artilleryman caught Gray's Skyraider in his gunsight reticle. He fired a stream of thirty-seven-millimeter shells toward the speeding naval plane, and one of the charges tore into the AD's engine. Flames erupted over Gray's cowling. Instinctively, one of his wingmen transmitted the dreaded message back to the ship: "Snow White has been hit!"

Gray zoomed to altitude and turned his bomber toward the sea and the *Essex*, fifty miles away. He quickly discovered that when he pulled back his fuel mixture control lever (located with the throttle and propeller controls on the port console), thus shutting off the flow of gasoline to the engine, the blaze went out. Of course that also caused the engine to stop. But by manipulating the mixture intermittently he was able to fly a little, glide a little, fly a little, glide a little.

Pilots dressed for the Korean winter and standing by for the call to the flight deck are, right to left, sitting, Paul Gray, skipper of VF-54, and wingmen, Sam Samples, now an American Airlines pilot, and Ken Shugart, who became a rear admiral. Behind them is Al Masson, now owner of "The Beach House," a French restaurant in New Orleans. (Gray)

In this manner he guided his aircraft over the mountains and plains and reached the water where the temperature was 35 frigid degrees.

"At that temperature you could freeze to death, even with an exposure suit on, in less than half an hour," said Gray. "Indeed, gloveless hands would be useless in five minutes." (Anti-exposure garments called "poopy" suits by the flyers, covered the body from neck to feet and were worn over thermal underwear. They were made of waterproof, rubber-type materials and were tightly sealed at the wrists. Large boots were actually integrated with the suit and were part of it.)

Gray spotted an American destroyer moving slowly through the churning sea and descended toward it. He ditched in the vicinity of the ship, extricated himself from the disintegrating airplane, and slipped into the sea. The inferno that was the R-3350 was quenched by the briny ocean.

That was shoot-down number three.

Some weeks later Gray was hit again but managed to limp into K-15, another emergency landing strip south of the 38th parallel, for shoot-down number four. Some people were beginning to believe that VF-54's skipper led a charmed life.

North Korea didn't look at it that way. Newspaper accounts began to mention the exploits of Snow White and his entourage of naval pilots who were scoring heavily against bridges, trains, trucks, and supply emplacements.

Take the attack on Kap Son, for instance. An enemy base constructed at the foot of a mountain slope near the Yalu River in North Korea, it became the focal point for one of the most daring raids of 1951, if not the whole war.

Intelligence sources had learned that a high-level meeting between North Korean and Chinese Communist officials was to take place there. Gray was selected to lead an attack against the base, a perilous 300 miles from the *Essex*. He and his wingmen would have to go without cover from friendly jet fighters.

After examining charts and analyzing the displacement of triple A

Creating vapor circles with its prop, a VF-54 AD rolls down the *Essex*'s wooden deck on combat mission, November 1951.

Skyraider

(anti-aircraft artillery) and radar detection sites, he decided to take his flight in low. The plan was to rendezvous after the launch, go feet dry (cross the coast line), and descend to tree-top height, skimming over the rugged terrain which, hopefully, would conceal the aircraft from the probing radar eyes of the enemy. Eight Skyraiders and eight Corsairs, heavily loaded with 1,000-pound bombs and napalm, were catapulted from the *Essex* in snowy weather. Formed into a loose cruise formation, the sixteen heavily-laden planes began their journey.

Navigation at low altitude (in later years such flights would be called "sandblowers") is difficult enough even over familiar ground because the pilot's perspective is radically different from that which he experiences at altitude. Careful preflight planning combined with precise timing and relentless tracking along the proscribed route are critical.

About an hour and a half after leaping from their mobile runway, Snow White and his troops spotted the target—principally a collection of closely spaced, simple, barracks-type buildings. Gray signaled his wingmen to add power for the run-in.

A stunned and bewildered gathering of Chinese and Koreans heard the thunder of sixteen piston-driven powerplants, then saw the wave of planes homing directly toward them.

"Stand by for the pull up," transmitted Gray over the intercom as he approached a preselected initial point.

His wingmen followed Gray in fanlike progression as he pulled his Skyraider steeply skyward, trading airspeed for altitude. Peaking out over the encampment at about 5,000 feet, he banked sharply, pushed the nose over, and dove down. One after the other the Skyraiders and Corsairs followed, releasing their weapons in sequence and racing away to clear the target area.

The first assault lasted only a minute or two but produced a holocaust of orange-red balls of fire followed by a towering display of brown-black, debris-filled clouds. Repeated runs using 500 pounders and then napalm completely burned and leveled the site.

"The beauty of it," remembered Gray, "was that not one bomb hit outside of a city block square. Every one was on target." Days later intelligence sources reported that the attack was extremely successful and that 510 of the enemy were killed. There were no American losses.

Shortly thereafter the word was passed that the North Koreans were offering $10,000 for heads of a naval pilot named Paul Gray and his wingmen.

Gray led ADs and F4U Corsairs on an attack on the heavily defended bridges at Toko Ri, shown here.

"That's a lot of money today and was a helluva lot more back then," said Gray. "I was flattered in a way, despite how disquieting it is to know someone has put a price on your person. This action also influenced my thinking in that if I were hit I would try, if at all possible, to avoid bailing out over land risking capture. I would take my chances with the sea."

It was no surprise when superiors began to notice signs of fatigue in Snow White. He developed what someone called a nervous twitch. The *Essex*'s flight surgeon told him he ought to step down for a while and rest. In fact, it was decided to officially ground him, which meant his complete removal from the flight schedule.

"It was a terribly cold winter morning," recalled Gray. "The wind was strong and laced with ice as it whipped across the flight deck.

Skyraider

But I was airborne and on the way to the target before the word was passed to me that I wasn't supposed to fly."

North of a place called Munchon, Gray was executing a strafing attack when .50-caliber ground fire ripped into his plane. Parts of the propeller blades were shot away. Despite this he managed to get the plane over water. The Skyraider vibrated horribly en route, and Gray was destined for another arcticlike dip in Wonsan Harbor. He crashed into roiling whitecaps.

Snow White was down again. The message was received in grim silence throughout the carrier. Squadron mates in the ready room paused in their card games. Five times Commander Gray had ridden a Skyraider down to earth or ocean. People were thinking, "The odds can't be with him this time."

And yet they were. The destroyer, the USS *Twinning*, hurried alongside the stricken flyer forty minutes after he crashed. The ship dispatched a crew in a rescue boat and retrieved Snow White from the freezing deep. The card games resumed. A wit in the group drafted a sign that was posted in the ready room: "Use Caution When Ditching Damaged Airplanes in Wonsan Harbor. Don't Hit Commander Gray."

That was the last time Gray crashed in an airplane, but it was not his last mission. He did take a rest as ordered but went on to fly ten more combat hops before the *Essex* was finally relieved on station and sent home.

"The thing about that war that lingers long in the mind," said Gray, "was the cold weather. Korea is a raw and forbidding land to begin with. Add frigid winds, snow storms, ice storms, and always the dark and unforgiving sea, and you have an environment far from conducive to flying. At the same time, the Skyraider was able to conquer the elements. It held up courageously in the face of terrible conditions. I went down in five of them, which I'm not exactly proud about. But the AD served me well, no doubt about it."

Gray took part in another critical raid, one that was eventually fictionalized in the book (and later the film) *The Bridges of Toko Ri*. Its author, James Michener, was a correspondent during the war and spent time aboard the *Essex*. He gained considerable background material and inspiration from people like Gray and Marshal Beebee, Gray's air wing commander, to whom Michener dedicated the book.

The Toko Ri bridges were located west of Wonsan in the central part of North Korea and served as a junction point for major southbound arteries—two railroad lines and a highway. These lines were vital to North Korea's supply chain. They were also heavily defended. The railroads paralleled each other as they passed down through sharply rising escarpments before crossing the frozen river and entering a flat stretch of land near the village of Toko Ri. The road bridge was oriented in the same direction as the railroad lines but was about 500 meters away.

Said Gray, "Pre-strike reconnaissance photos and intelligence sources revealed there were 58 gun emplacements arranged in groups of four, each group supported by a single radar unit. We spent quite some time in scull sessions and decided it was best to arm the 2,000 pounders—called 'Big Bombs'—we were to carry with VT (proximity) fuzes. These contained a miniature radio transmitter which activated the bomb when it sensed it was close to the ground or target. In other words, the weapon would explode microseconds before actually striking its target. We figured to achieve better results this way."

Gray led the flight which consisted of eight ADs and eight F4U Corsairs. (While the Corsair was designed as a fighter, it was versatile enough to adapt to the attack bombing mission.) Photo reconnaissance aircraft preceded the props into the target area to obtain pre-strike pictures.

"It was a well-planned mission," said Gray. "We went in high, at 15,000 feet. Each of us was tasked with hitting a specific gunsite. The strategy was to suppress the guns first with one group of planes, after which the remaining ADs and F4Us followed and went after the bridges. The plan worked. All but one gunsite were ultimately silenced. We knocked down the bridges. Three planes were shot down."

Still, while Kap Son and Toko Ri personified carefully planned and executed strikes, they were atypical of the Skyraider's combat role in Korea in the sense that most of its missions involved armed reconnaissance with emphasis on targets of opportunity. The AD, with its great range and ordnance-carrying capacity, was ideal for such endeavors.

Oddly, Paul Gray, the consummate aviator, preferred the "eyeball-to-eyeball" combat he experienced in Vietnam to his aerial battles. "In the air," he said, "you are remote from things. Its rather impersonal. On the ground its very personal."

Despite the fire and ice that characterized his experiences in the Orient during three bloody conflicts, that part of the world held a special appeal for Gray. After his naval career he returned to the Far East, spending ten years as a businessman in Tokyo where he

Paul Gray in retirement, 1980.

mastered the Japanese language. He fully retired in 1980 to San Marcos, California.

Like the Skyraider he flew, Paul Gray was a durable warrior who packed a solid punch and seemed almost at home in a hail of bullets and anti-aircraft artillery.

He said once, "I must admit, I loved combat." If the Skyraider could talk, perhaps it would choose the same words.

Torpedoes were used in Korea once, and once again Lieutenant Commander Carlson, of "Carlson's Canyon," and his VA-195 Skyraiders were involved. Their target: the sluice gates of the Hwachon reservoir, located in east central Korea. The enemy was using the vast waters of the reservoir as a weapon of sorts. By raising the gates they could flood "downstream" rivers, impeding UN soldier movements. Conversely, they could dam the waters and lower the levels of the rivers allowing easier transit by their own forces. EUSAK, Eighth U.S. Army in Korea, issued the orders to Task Force 77: "Destroy the dam."

With Corsairs in company for flak suppression, ADs dropped 2,000 pounders on the dam on 30 April 1951, but caused minimum damage. Next day, the ADs returned with a new twist, torpedoes. Carrier Air Group Commander, Commander R. C. Merrick, flew one of the squadron's AD-4s in section with Skipper Carlson. They would make a two-plane, single-section run-in. They had to maneuver cautiously down through the hills surrounding the reservoir and were forced to make a short run-in, not conducive to accuracy but in this case necessary.

Other aircraft from the *Princeton* provided cover and suppressed the inevitable ground fire as the two pilots pressed their attack, firing a total of eight torpedoes.

Of the eight released, six ran true. Testimony to both the pilots' skill and the capability of the Skyraider, the mission was a decisive success. One flood gate located in the middle of the dam was destroyed. A hole about ten feet in diameter was created in another gate. The waters poured forth, and the Communist forces had a major repair job on their hands.

VA-195, incidentally, had a predilection toward using ordnance, like torpedoes, not commonly employed. The "Dam Busters" earned notoriety later on in the war, on 29 August 1952, when one of their pilots dropped a kitchen sink (disproving the adage that the Skyraider could carry everything but the kitchen sink) that was attached to a 1,000-pound bomb, on a target near Pyongyang. VA-25 copied the gesture and dropped a sink on a Viet Cong target in Vietnam in 1966.

If nothing else, the Able Dog proved in Korea that it was a rugged piece of hardware. Take the case of Ensign R. R. Sanders of VA-65 off the USS *Boxer* on 17 September 1950. He lost all oil pressure when the engine of his AD-4 was hit by small-arms fire. Expecting the power plant to quit at any second, he eased back on the stick, climbing to convert airspeed to altitude. At 3,000 feet the engine quit. He was five miles southeast of Seoul.

While Sanders may have felt an instant lump in his throat, not at all assuaged by the sight of the rough terrain and the sudden absence of engine noise, he kept his composure. Spotting a narrow, dirt road that ran fairly straight, he elected to crash land on it. He dropped the nose, clicked out the dive brakes, and took aim on a spot short of his intended point of landing.

As he was descending and turning to line up with the road, the horrifying spectre of a tree loomed directly before him. Sanders rapidly calculated that he had enough airspeed to zoom-climb over this obstacle, then drop back down. On the other hand, he believed the maneuver might force him off track so he would miss the road.

"I'm gonna go through the tree," Sanders said to himself. "I hope the AD can hack it." And so he did. And so it did.

The aircraft struck the one-foot-thick tree at the wing root and plowed powerfully onward. Sanders had about 135 knots of airspeed when the lower dive brake scraped onto the ground, followed immediately by the remainder of the plane which skidded 100 feet, sending up an angry cloud of dirt. The machine nosed up almost forty-five degrees from the horizontal, then fell back down, again not unlike a beached fish.

Unhurt, Sanders climbed out of the cockpit and started to walk off to safety. As he did, he was startled by a familiar sound. As if the Skyraider were reminding him that there was still some life in the stricken bird, the UHF radio was continuing to function. It was blaring out transmissions, loud and clear, as the dust settled around the plane.

Jerry Canaan, who retired as a captain, recalls an incident involving Ensign John Reynolds in the summer of 1951. "We were on a strike over North Korea when John was hit by antiaircraft artillery," said Canaan. "He immediately headed for the coastline and our carrier, the *Bon Homme Richard*. Just as he landed and caught a wire his engine froze. We later took a picture of John standing under his Skyraider with his head sticking up in the hole where an entire lower cylinder had been shot away. Not a bad testimony to the 'staying power' of that great old airplane."

Even more remarkable is the following tale:

One frigid predawn morning in early 1952 a Guppy version of the Skyraider with a pilot and two crewmen on board was positioned on the *Valley Forge*'s port catapult. At the controls was Lieutenant Commander William H. "Buck" Rogers, who ran up his engine on signal from the catapult officer. The AD, with its round radar pod (some have likened it to an inverted mushroom) on the bottom fuselage, throbbed mightily. After checking his instruments, Rogers flipped on the running lights, indicating he was ready to go. Something went wrong with the catapult, however. The hold-back fitting had broken loose, and the Skyraider began free-sliding along the ice-coated deck.

The pilot hit the brakes and hauled back on the throttle, hoping to stop the beast. But the AD had other intentions—it kept sliding. Rogers had no choice but to ram the throttle full forward and try to take off anyway. Alertly, he warned his crewmen, Raymond Frausto and Donald Backofen in the rear of the plane, that ditching was imminent. The AD lumbered off the end of the flattop and fell toward the darkened waters.

Rogers yanked up the landing gear handle and gingerly eased back on the stick. The R-3350 was laboring powerfully. The Guppy, heavily loaded with fuel, thudded onto the water and *pancaked* back into the air, sending up an eerie pattern of salt spray.

Skyraiders proved durable—and flyable—even when damaged. Lieutenant (Junior Grade) Edward Phillips of VA-195 in Carrier Air Group 19 aboard the USS *Princeton* examines what's left of his vertical fin following a strike south of Wonsan.

Somehow Rogers was able to nurse his machine along, in the dark, mere feet above the wave tops, until it gained more suitable flying speed. He saved the plane, his crew, and himself. Later, the Skyraider was examined. Except for a rather severe indentation of the mushroom, the AD was none the worse for wear!

The nature of their missions was such that sustaining damage from flak and small-arms fire became routine for Korean War flyers. Operating in the midst of the fray, the Skyraider was battered as much as any aircraft in the inventory. And because it was hit so often, especially in the early months of the war, there was discussion in some quarters back home concerning armor plate and its possible use on the Skyraider (a subject discussed in greater detail in Chapter 4).

In the meantime the attack bombers pressed on, were shot at, and were hit. Some samples:

>Glenn W. Ward, a junior VF-54 pilot, who later retired as a commander, remembered that Ken Shugart (at this writing a rear

Skyraider

admiral on active duty), a pilot in Paul Gray's division, almost bought the farm. Said Ward, "Shugart took a hit in the canopy one day that would have drilled him from ear to ear except at the moment the round struck, he had leaned forward to turn on his master armament switch." Perfect timing.

>Aviation Electronicsman James Nesbit was flying in the aft section of a USS *Boxer* AD-4N. He certainly could have used armor plate when a Communist round tore up through the bottom of his

Lieutenant (Junior Grade) William T. Barron of the *Philippine Sea*'s VA-95 points to hole, 18 inches in diameter, created by 37-millimeter shell. Fragments also made 200 smaller holes in aft section of the AD-4.

plane. The shell penetrated the fuselage, pierced his parachute, setting it on fire, and then careened off his cartridge belt, only to be deflected out through the side of the aircraft.

>Aviation Electronicsman Samuel O. Rash was on a mission over North Korea when his AD-4N came under fire. Rash felt a thud, subtle but unnerving, beneath him. "Sir," he transmitted over the intercom to his pilot, Lieutenant (Junior Grade) Robert W. Probyn, "I think I may have been shot."

Because there was no apparent injury, the flight continued routinely back to the USS *Bon Homme Richard*. After landing an inspection revealed a .60-caliber, steel-jacked bullet that had penetrated Rash's seat but expended itself in the chute he was sitting on.

>Lieutenant William L. Harris, Jr. was on his first mission and made a nice dive-bombing run on a hydroelectric plant north of Hungnam. He didn't realize he'd been hit by something until he got back to his carrier. Maintenance men found fragments of concrete in the cowling and wings, pretty much verifying the accuracy of his bomb drops. Harris earned a new nickname: "Cement Mixer."

>Lieutenant (Junior Grade) Carl B. Austin pulled up from a bombing run on a target near Kumson. Suddenly, his aircraft was rocked by an exploding thirty-seven-millimeter shell that scored a direct hit on his VA-195 Skyraider. Dazed by the accompanying flash of brilliant light, he felt the control stick whipped out of his hand.

For a few seconds Austin fought the elements for control of the bird. Austin won. He noticed that the fuselage, tail, and canopy of his Able Dog were riddled by shell fragments. Even the port aileron was blasted away. But the Skyraider held together long enough for him to fly to a friendly airstrip.

On the ground Austin looked closer at himself and his wounded flying machine. Shell fragments had penetrated the canopy, grazed his neck, and embedded themselves in his helmet. Next day, his aircraft patched up, the young officer, presumably without a headache, flew back to his ship, the USS *Princeton*.

>For a brief time in 1952, Lieutenant Commander Lynn "Duke" DuTemple, from VA-195, was called "The Whistler." He was completing his fourth bombing run on a railroad bridge near Hamhung in the eastern part of North Korea when his canopy shattered. Duke figured it was small-arms fire that produced the crazy pattern of cracked glass. He returned to the *Princeton*.

44

Skyraider

As he banked into the final approach, the landing signal officer, Lieutenant Roy Farmer, heard a whistling, shriek-like sound that sent ominous shivers up the spine. Farmer thought, "I don't know what his problem is, but if he gets to the blunt end I'm gonna cut him, anyway." (Translation: If he made it over the fantail, he would give him the landing signal.) Which he did. The AD-4 settled normally into the wires. Examination revealed the reason for the howling noise. A thirty-seven-millimeter shell, not small-arms fire, had torn through one of the propeller blades, creating a hole bigger than a softball, before it slammed into the side of and shattered DuTemple's canopy.

>Bill Buttlar, also of VA-195, had dropped a 2,000 pounder on a railroad locomotive near Wonsan. He was traveling at 300 knots plus in the pull-up and was banking away from the target when the control stick was abruptly yanked from his hand. The AD heeled over upside down.

Buttlar managed to right the aircraft and make an emergency landing on board ship. Ground fire had scored a direct hit on the twenty-millimeter ammo cans in his wing, causing them to explode. The force of the blast whipped the AD upside down, which is enough to age any combat pilot by a year or two. Still, the Skyraider, and Buttlar, endured.

>Aboard the *Boxer* in 1952 VA-65's Ensign William R. Videto was considered the leading authority on bullet holes. On a rail strike near Wonsan a thirty-seven-millimeter shell penetrated the fuselage of his AD-4 and exploded three feet behind his seat, knocking off the radio mast. Mechanics counted 117 holes in the machine ranging in size as large as basketball. With words straight from a western movie Videto said, "That shell had my name on it, but they had it misspelled."

>In 1952 VF-194 was flying Skyraiders from the *Valley Forge*. The squadron's skipper, Lieutenant Commander Robert S. Schreiber, earned the dubious nickname "Ichiban Flak-catcher." He returned from his forty-first mission, for example, with his aircraft damaged for the fifteenth time. That averages being hit on one of about every three flights. Not a comforting percentage.

>In the same year Lieutenant (Junior Grade) Jack Everling of VA-195 heard a loud pop while approaching a target. First he thought his engine was running rough because there'd been no sign of enemy fire. Just as he reached for the throttle to adjust power,

something struck his bird with enough force to jerk the stick out of his hand. He was indeed under fire. On the instrument panel the cover on the clock shattered. Shards of glass flew around the cockpit. Everling leveled off at 4,000 feet as his wingman slid in alongside to examine his machine.

"You've got a hole in the left elevator," said his wingman.

It was a hole all right, a large hole. Everling flew to the ship by holding the stick back and judiciously using trim tabs. Back on deck investigation showed that a rivet from the armor plating (some units had armor plate by 1952) behind his seat had blown out and struck the clock. The concussion from the explosion in his tail section had buckled the heavy plating. There were 200 holes in the Skyraider. Everling was actually able to stand up *through* the hole in the elevator.

For a brief time they were called "The Lucky Five." *Essex*-based Skyraider pilots from VA-55 in 1952, they were perhaps as lucky as they were courageous.

Lieutenant John Page's propeller was blown off on a close air support mission over the central front. He crash-landed a mere hundred yards behind UN lines and was saved. Lieutenant Jim Norton took a hit while on an armed reconnaissance mission, guided his Able Dog to sea where he ditched, and was rescued by the destroyer *Osbourne*. Lieutenant Tom Davenport ran into trouble over Tanchon and was hit by triple A. He ditched off the coast and was rescued by the destroyer *De Haven*. But Ensign Peter Moriarity and Lieutenant (Junior Grade) John Lavra had even more dramatic sea stories to tell.

Moriarity was the first *Essex* pilot to hit the silk over North Korea and return. On a rescue mission for a downed pilot, he was hit and had to go over the side. Unfortunately, he descended almost into the hands of two North Korean soldiers. One of the enemy men, an incredibly bad shot, emptied a revolver at Moriarity from only five feet away, missing with all six shots.

Seeing a chopper in the distance, Moriarity broke from his captors and ran like a halfback into the middle of a clearing, dodging rifle fire from another band of approaching Communist troops. The UN helicopter, flown by a daring Lieutenant Franke, took a half dozen hits but landed in the field. Moriarity clambered aboard and was hauled up and away to safety.

Lavra was attacking the Kojo hydroelectric plant when his Skyraider was hit and burst into flames. Burning like a torch, the AD

Skyraider

plunged to the earth. Lavra could hardly hear the cries of his wingman: "Bail out! Bail out!"

He passed through 3,000 then 2,000 feet. Finally, at 1,000 feet, though painfully burned, he freed himself from his seat harness and did bail out. He landed behind enemy lines and troops were quickly closing toward him. But miracle worker Lieutenant Franke also appeared, swooped down, collected the Skyraider pilot, and carried him to safety.

Peter Kilduff, a naval aviation buff and free-lance writer, told the story of Vice Admiral G. E. R. "Gus" Kinnear, II, when the latter was a lieutenant (junior grade) flying ADs in Korea with VA-45. The following quotation is from *The Hook*, the voice of the Tailhook Association (Winter issue, 1978):

Kinnear's experiences operating from *Lake Champlain* involved some hard, and often hairy work. The citation for (an Air Medal) . . . reflects one of the tougher aspects of combat flight ops. It reads in part:

". . . Finding himself thrown into a steep diving turn by jammed aileron controls, he succeeded in completing a recovery at an altitude of less than a hundred feet above the terrain, and effected a climb to a safe parachuting altitude . . . (where) . . . he elected to save the aircraft and, by sustained physical force and the lashing of the control stick with his flight scarf to the side of the cockpit, proceeded over 100 miles to an emergency air strip. . . . With the stick still lashed as securely as possible against the locked controls, (he) executed a successful wheels down landing with no damage to the aircraft, on an extremely narrow landing strip . . . ."

Now that's a piece of flying!

The U.S. Marine Corps operated the Skyraider for more than a decade beginning in the early 1950s. Three squadrons flew the bird in Korea: VMA-121, VMA-251, and VMC-1, the last-named outfit tasked with seeking out enemy radar with their -Q versions of the AD. But VMA-121 had the most combat experience with the attack bomber.

The squadron was a reserve outfit drilling regularly at Naval Air Station Glenview, near Chicago, when it was activated in mid-1951. Lieutenant Colonel A. Gordon, a regular officer, was its commanding officer. By the fall of that year VMA-121 was based at K-3, an airfield in Pohang-dong, South Korea, flying close air support and attack missions. It thus became the first Marine Corps squadron to experience combat in the Skyraider. Its principal task was to support leatherneck ground forces, and in doing that the squadron went after a variety of targets, often operating within close proxim-

Marine Corps AD-2 of VMA-121. (McDonnell-Douglas, Harry Gann)

ity of friendly troops. They carried an enormous amount of ordnance and dramatically measured up to their nickname, "The Heavy Haulers." The flyers of VMA-121 liked to call the AD "Old Faithful." Their skipper, tragically, was killed in combat, as his aircraft exploded after takeoff. It was believed that saboteurs had infiltrated the Marine compound and caused the ensuing crash.

The Korean winter was as hard, if not harder, on the Marines ashore as it was for their counterparts on board the carriers. Temperatures of 35 degrees below zero were not uncommon at places like K-3. At night the nose portions of the aircraft were draped with heavy quilted covers.

Gas-operated pre-heaters piped hot air through special ducts into the aircraft's vital parts, warming ignition, hydraulic, oil, and fuel systems. VMA-121 technicians even built "nose hangars," which were like canvas-walled huts and were used to shield the forward section of the planes from icy winds. Combined with the pre-heaters, the nose-hangars made the mechanics' work a little easier and served to prevent frostbite. A major headache in the continuing struggle with the elements resulted from radical temperature changes when the engines and related systems cooled in the fierce low temperatures of night after running hot on missions during the day.

The Marine Corps AD pilots earned a reputation for heavy hitting in Korea. They consistently left the pierced-steel-planking airfields with enormous loads. VMA-121, which was part of Marine Air Group 12 in 1952, once launched ten Skyraiders on a single strike mission. Collectively, they carried thirty tons of ordnance. The largest reported load carried by a Marine Corps AD on another occasion consisted of three 2,000 pounders and a dozen 250 pounders—a mighty 9,000 pounds of bombs!

Able Dog and other pilots, quite obviously, had no trouble noticing the increased anti-aircraft artillery as the war wore on in Korea. Just as happened in Vietnam more than a decade later, the Communists built up their defenses enormously. Second-tour pilots, those who had flown combat missions in 1950, felt that groundfire in some areas had intensified tenfold by the end of 1951. And it continued to worsen after that.

The main heavy gun used by the North Koreans was the Soviet-built eighty-five-millimeter. Mounted on a mobile platform, it could fire twenty-pound projectiles up to 25,000 feet at a rate of fifteen to twenty a minute. The thirty-seven-millimeter automatic weapon, also mobile, fired a smaller projectile but at 160 rounds per minute.

In the spring of 1951 the North Koreans had about a thousand of these weapons. Two years later that number had nearly doubled. But mid-1952 all the key interdiction targets identified by strategic planners were considered to be heavily defended. Areas like "Death Valley," the route between Wonsan and Pyongyang, were especially well defended.

All the success stories notwithstanding, the AD loss rate in the first two years of fighting was alarming. Complicating matters was the fact that the AD-4 production line was scheduled to close down in the summer of 1952. Fortunately, a naval officer in the Bureau of Aeronautics was hard at work to correct the dilemma (see Chapter 4).

In any event, by the autumn of 1952, Rear Admiral Apollo Soucek, Commander of Task Force 77, ordered all pilots to bottom out at 3,000 feet in their dive-bombing runs. This reduced exposure to gunfire at an acceptable decline in bombing accuracy.

Importantly, for every flyer whose AD was maimed or torn asunder, there were half a dozen or more ground crewmen to mend the machines. Metalsmiths in particular got a workout in Korea. There were many chief petty officers like Orland G. Roney of VA-155's "Red Busters" aboard the *Princeton* who led the way.

One of his squadron's planes was so badly damaged by triple A that officers wanted it offloaded. "It'll take months to repair aboard ship," said one.

Chief Roney examined the bird carefully. "We can do it," he said. "we can patch her up." Somehow the higher-ups were persuaded to give the chief and his crew a try. Through the use of makeshift tools, sections of fuselage skin, patience, and a great deal of imagination, the Skyraider was flying again in seven days. Talk to any AD pilot, and he will never hesitate to extol the men like Roney who kept the aircraft flying. Their efforts are intrinsic to the Skyraider heritage.

Skyraiders, it should be noted, were not dedicated solely to the war in Korea during the early fifties. Flyers and enlisted personnel had their hands full on the other side of the world, too. In 1953 a Skyraider pilot from VA-15 based aboard the Mediterranean-deployed USS *Franklin D. Roosevelt* had to land wheels-up in a Greek cornfield. Shortly before crash-landing he transmitted a distress call. When the dust had settled, the uninjured pilot climbed out of the machine and was soon surrounded by curious farmers and other local citizens. Since the Greeks understood no English and he knew no Greek, the flyers used hand gestures to explain his predicament. Happily, the natives were friendly.

As was the custom of many flyers in those days—and perhaps is today as well—the pilot carried no wallet and was therefore broke. Wearing flight coveralls and scuffed boots, he hitched a ride to Larissa, forty miles away, where the Greeks had an air force base. He was advised to wait for the *Roosevelt* to dock in Salonika, some 85 miles distant.

Meanwhile, in response to the pilot's emergency radio message, the carrier had dispatched a team of eight men including an officer in charge plus mechanics, elecronicsmen, and metalsmiths. These men borrowed a truck and a mobile crane. The USS *Coral Sea*, also cruising in the Mediterranean, had sent in a tow-bar. About twenty-five Greek airmen joined the effort, and the two-nation task force set out for the cornfield. Salvage operations began.

The airplane was hoisted up by the crane so that the gear could be extended, and soon the bird was ready for towing. But the entou-

Skipper of the "Wolfraiders" of Marine Air Group 12, Lieutenant Colonel Wayne M. Cargill, right, discusses ordnance load with ground crewmen before combat hop in Korea. (McDonnell-Douglas, Harry Gann)

rage had proceeded only about a mile before the OinC ordered a halt. The conversation went something like this:

"Do you have a map of the area?" he asked one of the Greeks who knew a little English.

"No map has ever been made of this area," was the reply.

"OK," said the OinC, "We'll have to do our own measuring."

Whereupon he directed his men to measure the width of roads, streets, and buildings along the route to determine if the Skyraider could make it through following the intended course.

It couldn't.

"We'll have to go the long way around," sighed the OinC.

The group thus set out on a circuitious, fifty-five-mile route to Larissa, a route characterized by gullies, valleys, and hills. The Skyraider was a startling sight to the countrymen along the way. It was like a monstrous, mechanized warrior, attended devotedly by loyal legionnaires wearing blue dungarees and Greek khaki. At one point the men took to sticks and shovels and hacked away the sides of two hills so that the Able Dog could get by.

Their Greek Air Force counterparts helped in the endeavor. Yet they marveled at the Americans' disdain for post-lunch siestas. Exacerbating the task was the 90-degree heat. That first day the men toiled under the searing sun for fifteen hours before retiring to a hotel in Larissa. There, exhausted, the navy men were baffled by the menu in the dining room until an accommodating innkeeper led them directly to the kitchen where the troops pointed out their choices of cuisine.

Next day they towed, dug, cut away the earth, and even bridged a small stream, moving the Skyraider along. The bridge of another stream had railings too high to allow passage of the attack bomber. Rocks and boards were laboriously heaped on the center of the bridge to elevate the plane for travel over it.

When confronted by a network of power and telephone lines that would surely get entangled in the aircraft's already bent propeller blades, the Greek authorities cut the lines down. The plane passed through, and the wires were spliced back into operation.

The arduous routine continued for four days, at the end of which the Able Dog and its friends triumphantly entered the compound at the Larissa air base. Even the AD looked tired. It was covered with dirt. Its tires were worn. The bent prop gave it a forlorn appearance.

But a new propeller was flown in and installed, and the bird was carefully checked and made ready for flight. A quarter of a million dollars' worth of Skyraider was back in the inventory. And some American sailors—diplomats in dungarees—not only had made some Greek friends, but demonstrated in the truest sense that where there's a will, there is a way.

About the time of the Larissa episode a *Midway*-based pilot from VA-25, Lieutenant James H. Snow, developed a rough-running engine and landed on a small airstrip 450 miles deep in central Turkey, at a place called Cukurhisar. Needing an engine change, Snow lived with the leader of the local village while awaiting a replacement power plant. He visited schools, learned to like the food, and participated in village festivities.

Since neither he nor his hosts understood each other's language, there were many animated, frustrating, and often comical exchanges of hand and arm signals.

A maintenance crew finally arrived and was able to change the engine in two days. Snow's sojourn had lasted a memorable and enlightening fourteen days. He roared off the Cukurhisar runway and flew the AD 1,700 miles back to the *Midway*, which was in port in Cannes in the South of France.

Meanwhile, back in Korea, not only was the attack bomber durable under fire, it served diverse purposes, sometimes to the chagrin of the maintenance officers and the mechs. During "Operation Pinwheel," ADs aligned on the bow were used to help the carrier maneuver when in port by producing an artificial wind force à la R-3350s. The strain on the power plants was considerable, but the method worked. An example:

The *Bon Homme Richard* was moored to a buoy in the harbor of Sasebo, Japan, when it began to swing rapidly to port toward a British ship, HMS *Ceylon*, which for some reason was not swinging with the tide. The buoys of both ships were far enough apart to allow the vessels to pass safely if both swung simultaneously. But because the *Ceylon* wasn't moving, a collision was imminent. Flight quarters was sounded, and crewmen manned eight Skyraiders parked at the corners of the flight deck forward, facing inboard. Their engines were quickly fired up.

The swing was checked when the two ships were a few feet apart. The *Bon Homme Richard*'s stern was then swung around to starboard, and a good number of people wiped the sweat from their brows. The British cruiser was expeditiously moved to another berth. Although the strain on the R-3350s was bothersome to the Skyraider people, Operation Pinwheel did have its value.

So, the AD was useful at times, even when it was sitting down. Take the case of Carrier Air Group 102 headed by Commander H. W. Fink aboard the *Bon Homme Richard* in the early 1950s. The group consisted of Naval Air Reserve squadrons flying Corsairs, Panthers, and Skyraiders. One of its F9Fs was forced down at an auxiliary airstrip. Repairs were made, but there was no twenty-eight-volt DC starting unit available to ignite the jet engines. Without that power the Panther would have to stay right where it was.

CAG Fink got together with Lieutenant Commander Don Webb and Lieutenant L. A. Bailey, the maintenance officer and electronics expert, respectively. Eyeing one of the ship's AD-4Qs, Bailey got the idea that the Skyraider's two NEA-5 generators, functioning in parallel, could produce the needed twenty-eight volts. Each generator was rated at 200 amperes, and two in parallel could furnish 400 amps. He believed that a 100 percent overload needed to furnish the required amps for starting the jet could be achieved if only for a short period. (The power required for operation of the Panther's starter fell off rapidly after the initial start and was within the amount the two generators could be expected to furnish.)

The AD was flown to the emergency strip along with a cable rigged to channel the power from the two generators directly from a common bus to the power outlet receptacle on the F9F. The cable was connected, and the Skyraider was turned up to 1,900 rpms. Like a blood transfusion, power flowed from the piston aircraft to the jet, which was fired up without any adverse effects. Score one for the Able Dog.

In a rather unique undertaking, Guided Missile Unit 90 operated AD-4Qs on some "drone" missions in Korea in August 1952, once again demonstrating the Skyraider's extraordinary adaptability. Flying from the USS *Boxer*, six attacks were made. Grumman-built F6F-5K Hellcat drones, loaded with a single 2,000-pound bomb each, were configured with television devices that gave the "mother" planes, the Skyraiders, a picture of where they were heading. One AD launched from the port catapult ahead of the drone. A second AD, positioned aft between the two catapults, controlled the drone as it was launched from the starboard cat. The first Skyraider then took over and guided it to the inland target for the attack. One successfully hit target was a railway bridge at Hungnam.

A full-scale war like the Korean conflict—although not a global affair—is a twenty-four-hour-a-day operation. Whereas the Skyraider was an ideal platform for daytime combat, it could be argued that it was even more effective after dark. No group of flyers played a more important role in the fighting than those who went into the combat skies after the sun went down. These were the men of the "night shift," to whom we next turn our attention.

One of the naval reserve squadrons called up for combat in Korea was VA-702. Here, one of the unit's ADs bores in on a railroad bridge with some spans already knocked away. Craters testify to previous bomb impacts.

◄ Production line at El Segundo.

Gray's Skyraiders put a bend in this rail line with accurate bombing. (Gray)

Damaged bridge.

North Koreans didn't sling arrows at ADs as this photo might indicate. Actually, one of Gray's men plugged an authentic bullet hole with the "Indian Missile" as a joke. (Gray)

This AD-3 made it back to the *Valley Forge* despite fuselage badly punctured by enemy fire. Aviation Technician First Class Clifford E. Cameron, left, and Lieutenant Commander Jerry Lake were on board at the time.

VA-195 earned its title "The Dambusters" when Lieutenant Commander Swede Carlson, C.O., and Carrier Air Group Commander R. C. Merrick successfully launched torpedoes from their AD-4s against Hwachon Dam in May 1951. Views are from reservoir side of the dam; beyond the dam; and of the Skyraiders pulling up after the run as depicted by R. G. Smith, one of aviation's greatest artists.

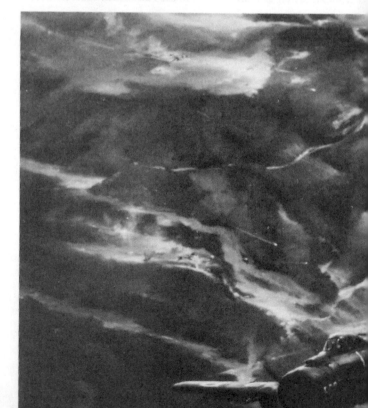

Korean winter was brutal on both men and machines. Here, troops shovel snow on flight deck.

This Skyraider had trouble landing and nosed up when wheels got entangled in barrier wires.

In another flight deck mishap this AD lost its engine, but pilot emerged intact.

Pilot survived malfunctioning catapult shot.

Carrying a mixed ordnance load, VA-728 AD awaits launch aboard the USS *Antietam*, January 1952.

Bridle is attached to VA-75 Skyraider loaded for bear, aboard the *Bon Homme Richard*, December 1952.

Formation of VMA-121 Skyraiders. (McDonnell-Douglas, Harry Gann)

AD-4Bs had nuclear capability. This one was used at China Lake, Calif., for experimental work. Here it releases a torpedo during a test.

◀ Winter conditions plagued the Korean carriers, but weather didn't very often stop VC-35 from their night work.

Commander Ettinger in cockpit of VA-25 Skyraider when he was C.O. of the squadron in Vietnam aboard the USS *Midway*, 1965. (Ettinger)

Ettinger is in number 04 in this formation of AD-4NLs. He was piloting number 03 when s▮
down. (Ettinger)

Hank Suerstedt, C.O. of VF-54, in Skyraider cockpit. (Suerstedt)

An F4U Corsair rests among a forest of ADs on the flight deck. Recognizing that the Navy was losing its Skyraiders at an excessive rate in combat, Suerstedt took corrective action.

A railroad train and a round-house, like this one smashed by VA-55 1,000 pounders in late 1952, were valued targets in Korea.

After a strike against Red targets, VA-75 pilots from the *Bon Homme Richard* engage in some "tail chase" flying.

VF-194 ADs aboard the USS *Boxer*, in port, Yokosuka, Japan, 1953.

3

Night Shift

The rest of us dutifully followed. And followed. And followed. Turned out the guy had picked up a star and was waiting for the star to turn downwind.

Lieutenant (Junior Grade) Harry Ettinger,
describing FCLP at San Diego

If there is one evolution that sets carrier pilots apart from all others, it is landing aboard the flattops in the dark. When naval aviators were fitted with special measuring devices to calculate the strain and anxiety they experienced during night combat missions in Vietnam, they were found to feel more pressure during the landing sequence than they did when over the beach in a hostile environment.

Carrier pilots were not astonished at this. They knew—and know—that flying an airplane in the night landing pattern is never less than a test of their total capabilities. This is so even when the weather is CAVU—clear with visibility unlimited. Throw in heavy seas, a heaving deck, poor visibility, and gusty winds, and the evolution demands every ounce of their skill, experience, and determination.

The reason: put simply, the pilot must concentrate on two moving objects, the ship and the plane, and ensure that they meet each other at a precise point, on a precise airspeed, and at a precise rate of descent, without benefit of visual cues such as the horizon, which during daylight hours help him maintain a safe orientation with the earth. In the space of a few critical moments he must continuously scan back and forth between a field of instruments in the cockpit,

VC-35 operated AD-4NLs as well as AD-3s like the one in the lead here; and AD-42Qs, following the -3, as depicted in this October 1950 picture.

73

their faces bathed in red light, and the ship beyond, distinguished from its black surroundings by a seemingly pitiful paucity of white lights. In between lies the dark no-man's-land of sea and sky, an almost alien mass of nature's elements. He must glance at the ship, then his instruments, the ship again, and so on. He must make instant judgments and therefore instant corrections. He must manipulate the throttle, stick, and rudder controls in a relentless effort to stay on the glide path. As he nears the seaborne runway, he receives helpful instructions by radio from "Paddles," the landing signal officer. Nowadays, unlike the early fifties when it was a matter between the pilot and Paddles alone, he also eyeballs a landing signal mirror, or Fresnel lens, with its orange "meatball" aligned between two rows of green datum lights that extend outward from the nine and three o'clock positions of the mirror. This gives him glide path information. Yet, even with the computerized autopilots and sophisticated landing systems of the 1980s, night carrier landings are seldom routine.

Perhaps the most unsung heroes of the Korean War, then, were the flyers who worked the night shift, the men who flew the mission and recovered back aboard, all between the hours of sunset and sunrise, on a continuing, night-in, night-out basis. Among the night flyers, AD drivers were prominent. Not only did they undergo the stress of taking off and landing in the dark, they went directly in harm's way between these two evolutions.

A critical part of stateside training was FCLPs—field carrier landing practices, especially at night. Lieutenant (Junior Grade) Harry Ettinger described the evolution: "We had six planes in the pattern at Ream Field, San Diego. It was fairly realistic because we'd launch, pass some sand dunes, and then be over the water. The key to a good pattern was to commence your turn downwind when the aircraft ahead of you was 45 degrees off your nose. You had to concentrate because the skies could play tricks on you as you focused on the lights of other planes.

"One night," remembered Ettinger, "there were six of us flying the oval-shaped pattern. The sky was clear and studded with stars. After a few passes one of the fellows on his climb-out picked out what he thought was the aircraft in front of him and obediently emulated his track. The rest of us dutifully followed. And followed. And followed. Turned out the guy had picked up a star and was waiting for the star to turn downwind. We ended up ten miles out to sea before a voice on the radio quipped, 'This is your friendly LSO. Would you mind coming back to the field, boys?'"

Which leads to Ettinger's perspective on night carrier landings: "I've always felt that throughout my military career 80 percent of the flying was pure labor and rather boring. About 15 percent was stimulating and uplifting. I loved those minutes in the sky. The remaining five percent was sheer panic. I'm referring, of course, to night 'traps,' especially those on the straight deck carriers of the early 1950s."

Because of the potential submarine threat, carriers used minimum lighting at night. In addition to the red truck light located at the highest point on the masthead, the pilot had only pin and dust pan lights outlining the landing portion of the deck for guidance—and these weren't visible until planes were in the groove on final approach. (Dust pan lights provided a dim impression of the deck edge; pin lights were set into the deck and covered, outlining the runway.)

Said Ettinger, "We'd break at 300 feet, using the Fox Corpen (ship's advertised course [as a guide]), dirty up (extend wheels, flaps and tail hook), turn downwind and descend to 90 feet working airspeed back to 90 knots. We had radar altimeters which helped, but on black nights you needed all the assistance you could get. Abeam the truck light you started the turn. When you reached the 45 degree position the LSO entered the act. He began signaling with his paddles—tennis racket-type devices held in both hands. The LSOs wore fluorescent coveralls and the paddles were outlined with strips of similar material. If you didn't pay attention to the Fox Corpen and adjust your pattern accordingly, matters got complicated, and you had to make too many adjustments causing a bad approach and, in all likelihood, a wave-off.

"Frankly," Ettinger went on, "I always saw a purple shadow at the 45 rather than the LSO. I don't know how else to explain it. I could only see that purple shadow, even though there was a black light shining on his fluorescent outfit to illuminate him. When I was about 200 feet from the blunt end of the ship I was finally able to make him out. Once 'connected' to him, you were all hands and feet, flying the airplane, obeying his visual signals, making every humanly possible effort to get squared away for touch down on the still nearly invisible flight deck.

"As you neared the cut point, the dust pan and pin lights came on. Before you knew it, the LSO signaled you to chop the throttle and make your landing. As soon as you caught the wire, all the lights went out again. The feeling was: 'God, I got that one out of the way.' But the episode wasn't over yet. Next, you eyeballed the taxi direc-

Mighty Mouse 2.75-inch rockets are fired during tests in February 1950, by Skyraider from unit based at Inyokern, California. VC-35 was the first squadron to use the rockets in night combat.

tor's yellow wands, not him because you simply couldn't see him, just those wands which were like mysterious lights with a life of their own, dancing in the dark.

"Since we were usually the last planes to recover for the day, we had to be rushed below so that the crew could ready the 'daylight' aircraft for morning operations. We'd follow those dancing wands and taxi onto the side elevator which to me was another experience in horror. I always had the sensation as I moved precariously onto the elevator that one of the wheels would go over the side and catastrophe would follow. I would look down from the cockpit, see the wake of the ship which produced an eerie, phosphorescent glow, and struggle to maintain equilibrium. I suppose this was one of the reasons that aviation candidates had to pass spatial orientation tests before being allowed to fly.

"The yellow wands then told you to spin the AD around, nose facing inboard. You'd get an emergency stop signal immediately followed by the inevitable and abrupt plunge to hangar deck level. You would go down. The aircraft would go down. But your heart stayed right up there on the flight deck. Once you taxied forward into the hangar bay, the glow of red night lights made it seem bright as day. At last, for the first time in the whole macabre sequence, you felt comfortable again."

The night shift people used radar, with courageous enlisted men manning the scopes in the fuselage station of AD-4Ns and AD-4Qs, to probe their way through grimy and unsettling weather conditions. They dropped flares to illuminate targets, and bombs, rockets, and cannon fire to destroy them. The "nighthecklers," or "roadrunners," as they were sometimes called, contributed immensely to the allied interdiction effort. They were probably the best-trained combat aviators and aircrewmen in the world at the time.

One of the principal sources for the night shift was VC-35. (The C stood for Composite; the V, incidentally represents "heavier than air.") For nearly three years the San Diego-based unit sent seventeen teams, or splinter groups, to carriers in support of Task Force 77. The primary mission of VC-35 and its AD-4Ns was antisubmarine warfare. In practice, however, the majority of sorties were devoted to interdiction of rail and highway traffic at night. When they did fly ASW missions, they joined with counterparts from VC-11, which also functioned in small contingents aboard carriers, to form hunter–killer teams.

"Moonlight Sonata" and "Insomnia," for example, were night heckling operations under way in 1952. Assigned to harass a portion of a railway line, aircrews, often operating in two-plane sections, used bombs, napalm (especially effective because it lit up the target for continued attack runs), rockets, and cannon fire. The darker the night, the better, because the enemy would be forced to use lights to guide his rolling stock. Thus targets were a bit easier to pick out.

A typical ordnance load for a VC-35 AD-4N included full cans of twenty-millimeter, about 800 rounds total; a half dozen rocket packs with seven rockets in each (the 2.75-inch Mighty Mouse rockets, which VC-35 was the first squadron to use in night combat); a single 500 pounder; three 250 pounders; and four flares, each rated at about a million candlepower. A napalm cannister or more might be substituted for some of the bombs. The payload added up to about 3,000 pounds.

Team George of VC-35 aboard the USS *Oriskany* flew a mission that went as follows:

Haze hung over the Korean coastline on a cold murky night in April 1953. Lieutenant T. P. "Teeps" Owens was at the controls of his Skyraider with Petty Officers Third Class J. C. Peckenpaugh and

Skyraider

R. M. Rial operating the radar and occasionally glancing out their small fuselage window looking for North Korean activities along a section of railroad tracks.

When Owens spotted what appeared to be smoke rising from the track, he maneuvered his machine quickly and pickled off one of the parachute-retarded flares.

The powerful, pyrotechnic light glowed nightmarishly as it slowly descended. Nearing the ground, it illuminated an eight-wheeled locomotive pulling nearly twenty railway cars. An ideal find!

Three miles ahead was an associate heckler in an AD-4N assigned to monitor a separate section of the track nearby, Lieutenant T. G. McClellan. He also saw the flare. In anticipation of this, Teeps called his squadron mate.

"Hey Mac, I've got a good one," he transmitted excitedly. "Fly for the flare."

McClellan added power. His Skyraider quickly gathered speed. Over the intercom to his crewmen, F. B. Georges and E. L. Hazelwood, he reported, "Looks like Teeps got us a train. Here we go!"

Owens began attack runs, hitting a box car on his first try. It burst into flames. Enemy troops rapidly uncoupled the locomotive and began to make a run for safety, obviously trying to reach a tunnel farther down the track. Realizing this, Owens altered his attack. Despite the gloomy, scudlike clouds in the area, he was able to drop a bomb on the track itself. The engine, traveling fast now, plowed off the rails, nosed up crazily, and fell off on its side amid a cloud of smoke.

McClellan and his crew meanwhile were strafing the immobile freight cars, which had now become sitting ducks. Secondary explosions blossomed in the night as the cars burned. The mission itself was a resounding success. True enough, the tracks damaged on this night would be repaired within hours. And somehow the locomotive and its cars would be either fixed or replaced. This standoff of sorts was typical of the interdiction scenario.

While there were many nights, or portions of nights, when the Communists moved supplies undetected, the mere presence of night hecklers and roadrunners inhibited the southward flow of materials.

VC-35 teams operated in four-plane units. They flew from all but three attack carriers in the course of the fighting. It was a squadron rich in talent. Commissioned before the outbreak of hostilities in May 1950, it was ultimately manned by 650 enlisted personnel and a hundred officers. Most of the pilots were hand-picked World War II veterans averaging 1,000 flight hours.

Newly assigned VC-35 pilots first were instructed about the -4N and -4Q and their capabilities. Then came survivial training, followed by three intensive months of instrument and night flying combined with radar-controlled bombing at the Naval Air Station in Barber's Point, Hawaii.

Aircrewmen underwent equally tough training, learning not only regular duties common to aircrewmen in other aircraft, but how to operate and maintain the not-so-uncomplicated electronic gear in the -4N.

Enlisted personnel, incidentally, came from various rating groups. They were ordnancemen, mechs, electronicsmen, metalsmiths, and so on. Background mattered less than the desire to play a part in night attack work. They flew, but they also worked as much as possible in their own ratings when on the ground.

After the pilots honed their skills in Hawaii, they joined up with the aircrewmen. Teams studied antisubmarine warfare, close air support techniques, and electronics, and practiced bombing. Then they formed into groups of six officers and forty enlisted men with four airplanes. The entire training period usually took about eight months.

Above all else, the AD-4Ns, aided by radar, could poke through the weather and go where others couldn't, especially at night. They were a special breed.

They weren't supermen, however. One night in the winter of 1952 on board the *Valley Forge*, a team was awakened after midnight for an antisubmarine patrol. The weather was bad. It was snowing so heavily that visibility was measured in mere feet. The flyers figured their flight would surely be canceled. Nevertheless they went through the tedious ritual of briefing, climbing into their winter flight gear, and standing by. Certainly, the welcome call would come down from on high: "Cancel the launch!"

But the ready room squawk box crackled, "Pilots, man your planes." They were stunned. "They can't mean it," muttered one of them, referring to the sometimes nebulous powers above who called the shots.

Their wary expressions betraying their anxiety, the night shift, with aircrewmen obediently following, dutifully trudged up to the flight deck. As they emerged from the catwalk, they were pelted by whirling snowflakes. It was brutally cold as they stumbled across the deck, literally groping their way to the planes, stepping over tie-down chains and chocks, to reach their white-coated aircraft. The snow was coming down so thickly that even as deck crews swept away an accumulation, a new layer appeared almost instantly.

"They can't send us out in this," one flyer announced unconvincingly to a shipmate.

Yet there was no reprieve. The pilots and crew manned their machines. Ominously, an order boomed through the frigid night: "Start engines!" The AD-4Ns rumbled to life. After a few moments the catapult officer appeared, ready to go to work.

"We're good," thought one of the pilots, remembering his specialized training, his considerable store of experience, and the marvels of radar, "but this is a bit much."

The snow continued to cascade downward, enveloping the aircraft, the flight deck, the ship itself. Finally, the pilot of the AD-4N strapped into position on the bow decided to have a say in his destiny, a tinge of anger unmistakable in his voice.

"Uncle George, this is Crock One," he said. "For your information I am on the starboard catapult and in my opinion the weather is unsatisfactory."

A calm, deliberate voice from primary, the control tower in the island structure, sounded in his earphones.

"Crock One," it said. "This is Uncle George. Roger your message regarding weather on the starboard catapult. All planes will be launched from the port cat!"

There was a period of silence as the black humor of the remark settled in, whereupon the tension was decisively alleviated by the command: "Pilots, cut your engines! Your flight is canceled." Sighs of gratitude filled more than one cockpit that evening. Whoever the decision maker was, he took his own sweet time, but at lease his decree was a favorable one. The snow continued to fall as the flyers disembarked from their Skyraiders.

Harry Ettinger's team served on board the *Valley Forge*. Shortly after entering the combat zone, on 13 December 1951, he was piloting an AD-4NL (the L indicating a "winterized" version of the AD-4N) with radar operator AT2 Julian H. G. Gilliland and ECM man AD3 Jess R. McElroy aboard.

"We launched with another AD at 1550 to recce (conduct reconnaissance of) a route identified in tactical lingo as Green Four Tango," said Ettinger. "We were at 5,500 feet in trail on the leader, flying at 4,500 feet. We came to a large valley through which ran a

Lieutenant (Junior Grade) Harry Ettinger at the controls of an AD-4NL with air-crewmen Aviation Technician Second Class J. H. Gilliland and Aviation Mechanic Third Class Jess R. McElroy on board. Head of one of crew can be seen in window of fuselage access door. Gilliland and McElroy were with Ettinger when their aircraft was shot down in North Korea. (Ettinger)

railroad and a river. Suddenly, streams of 37-millimeter shells with tracers burst up from the ground. 'Get out of there,' I warned the leader. Apparently, he was having radio problems and didn't hear me. I decided to descend, picking up speed, to pull alongside and get his attention. The AAA continued, and we were hit. The shells exploded, rupturing the fuel tank or the fuel lines, maybe both. The plane burst into flames. All communications, including the inter-com were lost. Smoke filled the cockpit chamber. Instinctively, I turned toward the sea. I jettisoned the bombs, flares, and napalm we were carrying. I figured we were about 65 miles behind the front lines.

"I knew we had to get over an 8,700-foot-high peak in order to make it to the coast. But it didn't take long to realize we weren't going to make it. The smoke intensified and the engine began a sickening sputter. It would stop, run, then stop again. I worried about my troops in the back, not realizing that the flames had already consumed their compartment. I didn't know it right away, but they had jettisoned the doors on either side of the fuselage compartment and bailed out.

"I was flying perpendicular to the mountains, desending," said Ettinger. "They loomed bigger and bigger. I'd pass over one ridge into a valley, then another ridge, and another valley. The plane was getting hot. I rolled the canopy back and prepared to go over the side. My parachute or something got hung up as I tried to vacate the machine. In a half up, half down position I was able to see along the starboard side of the plane. I felt that Gilliland and McElroy had gotton out even though all that remained of the aircraft from the fuel tank aft were the ribs. I settled back trying to unhitch myself from whatever was binding me. As I did so, the Skyraider smacked into trees on top of a ridge. We busted through them out into an open valley. I remember saying to myself: 'It really is time to abandon ship.'

"I put one foot on the seat in a sort of crouched/standing position and with the other, kicked the control stick forward. To my immense relief I was popped out of the top of the aircraft. I hit the rudder sharply with my left leg, pulled the D ring and got a good chute. I swung up once, then down, like a pendulum, and hit the ground. I rolled 50 to 60 feet before coming to a stop. I was stunned but alive and discovered I was in a frozen rice paddy that was covered with six inches of snow. The Skyraider disappeared over the next ridge and crashed.

"I heard some shouting and as I started to shed my parachute," Ettinger continued. "I was struck in the head by a rifle butt. I looked up and saw a group of soldiers all trying to take a whack at me. I was severely beaten until one of their leaders came along and put a stop to it.

"I learned later that Gilliland had taken a piece of shrapnel in his left arm from the AAA. He landed amidst a large concentration of Chinese troops who fired at him as he descended, putting a slug in his leg before he landed. He was captured immediately. McElroy alighted among North Korean troops. I never realized it at the time, but when that shell exploded in our Skyraider, it blasted minute particles of shrapnel into our legs. It wasn't until 1953 that some of these little chips surfaced on our skin and we were able to pluck them out. In fact they kept appearing up to two years later."

Nevertheless, injuries and incarceration failed to subdue Harry Ettinger. He went on to become skipper of VA-25, flew Skyraiders in Vietnam, and eventually retired as a captain.

Testimony to VC-35's participation in the war is the fact that of twenty naval aviation personnel, pilots and aircrewmen, captured by the Reds and released in the summer of 1953, five were from the squadron. In addition to Ettinger, Gilliland, and McElroy, the five included AT1 Raymond L. Blazevic and Ensign (later Captain) Gerald C. Canaan.

Other VC units in Korea were VC-11, VC-12, and VC-33. They may have been splinter groups functioning in relatively small detachments, but the contingents from these squadrons, like the Skyraider, were durable, effective, and equal to their task.

4

Armor Plate
and Other Things

In view of the hostilities and significantly high combat attrition of ADs in Korea, I urge that immediate action be taken to initiate a new contract for additional AD aircraft.

> Letter sent to the chief of BuAer by Lieutenant Commander Hank Suerstedt, AD class desk and project officer in BuAer

Zapatero A Tus Zapatos. (Spanish for "Shoemaker, to your shoes.")

> Response to Suerstedt's letter by a senior plans officer in BuAer

The most radical departure from the basic Skyraider design was embodied in the AD-5, a model that, in the eyes of many, was the most useful Able Dog of all. It was a couple of feet longer than the "straights" and had a modified ventral fin. The major change, however, was an enlarged cockpit that permitted side-by-side seating for the pilot and a radar operator/navigator up front and two more seats aft for radar and electronics equipment operators.

The AD-5 featured the latest search radar and was modified to tackle the night, early-warning, and countermeasures missions. But because it was heavier than its predecessors with essentially the same power plant, it was a bit more sluggish to handle. Still, it was agile and maneuverable, as well as the most versatile member of the Skyraider family. The AD-5W flew for the first time on 17 August

AD-6s, like this one on an AD-5W's wing, were ordered in 1952. Like the AD-7 and the AD-5, however, the AD-6 did not enter combat until the 1960s in Vietnam. This picture was taken in 1956. When U.S. military aircraft underwent redesignation in 1962, the AD series became A-1s.

Skyraider

1951 but was not used in the Korean War. Its taste for combat was wetted some years later in Vietnam.

While the so-called conventional war flamed across an Asian peninsula called Korea, military planners were also occupied with a global "cold" war as the Soviets and the Americans continued to develope their nuclear arsenals. The AD-4B version of the Skyraider, flown in Korea and elsewhere, was configured to carry nuclear weapons as well as conventional ordnance. In 1952 the Navy ordered a number of AD-6s, which were considered advanced versions of the AD-4B. (The -6 and its final successor, the AD-7, which was much like the -6 except for a slightly more powerful R-3350 and strengthened wing fittings, would taste combat extensively in Vietnam. Throughout their lifespan they also maintained the capability of deliverying nuclear weapons over great distances.)

Thanks in part to Admiral "Bull" Halsey, there was a man in naval aviation's officer inventory who was instrumental in prolonging the life of the Skyraider during what might be called its mid-life crisis in Korea—when replacements were hard to get and losses continued to mount. Without his efforts and those of a few others who shared his strong feelings about the attack bomber, the -5, -6, and -7 models might have had a much shorter tour of duty.

Hank Suerstedt was skipper of Torpedo Squadron 100 as a twenty-five-year-old lieutenant commander in 1945. His outfit was part of Carrier Air Group 100 operating their TBM Grumman Avengers out of Naval Air Station Barbers Point, Hawaii. He and two other squadron commanding officers from the Air Group shared a house on the air station.

Late one Saturday afternoon, about an hour before they were to host a cocktail party at their house—to be followed by a large, formal soiree at the officer's club for shipmates and many civilian friends from Oahu—the three commanding officers were relaxing. They were sipping a last cold beer after wrapping up preparations for the major event. At this inopportune moment, an official sedan pulled up in front of the house bearing a naval officer who, although in uniform, looked like a transplant from a Madison Avenue executive suite.

"He was pompous as hell," remembered Suerstedt (pronounced sir´stet). "He came in and ordered, 'Everybody out! An admiral will be staying here tonight!'"

"We weren't having any of that," said Suerstedt. "The invitations for our party had been out for weeks. The booze and hors d'oeuvres were ready. Some of our VIP guests from Oahu were probably already on the way."

In terse, unequivocal language the three skippers advised the lieutenant commander precisely where he could place his "clear-out-now" order. Undaunted, Mr. Madison Avenue, obviously an aide to an admiral, repeated his message.

"What admiral wants our house?" asked one of the COs.

"Yeah," echoed another, "who's the wheel?"

"I'm not at liberty to say, but I've told you to leave," the officer said, whereupon he pivoted, got back into the sedan, and drove away, apparently hoping his warning would be heeded.

It wasn't. At least not until a couple of hours or so later when three cars in trail formation arrived at the front of the house. From one of the autos stepped a very imposing figure in khaki uniform.

Suerstedt and the others realized that Admiral William F. "Bull" Halsey himself was coming up the path. The old warrior came in, smiled, and asked where his room was. Within seconds the party came to a halt. There was a rapid, mass egress from the house and an early start at the officers' club where, happily, the party continued until the wee hours.

But at about 3 A.M., fueled by the events of the evening and other spirits, Suerstedt said to himself, "By God, I'm gonna sleep in my own bed tonight."

"I went back to the house," he recalled, "talked my way past a Marine guard posted at the door, and found my way to the kitchen. As was my practice after a long night of partying, I opened a can of tomato soup and started to whip up some eggs and toast. As I was preparing the food, squinting now and then to keep things in focus, an elderly gentleman wearing a blue bathrobe shuffled into the kitchen.

"'What're you having there, son?'" the man who was obviously Bull Halsey asked. 'Scrambled eggs, sir,' I said. 'Throw a couple in there for me, would you?' he asked. I said, 'Yessir,' and began cracking a couple of more eggs."

Continued Suerstedt, "The admiral's unpretentious manner was such that I began to feel at ease. We sat down, and as we ate he talked freely."

The conversation between one of the Navy's highest ranking officers—and aviators—and a youthful carrier pilot mellowed. Halsey asked Suerstedt if he was going to stay in the Navy after the war. Suerstedt explained that he was a reserve officer and that he feared that as an ex-reserve he would be discriminated against professionally by the regular Navy organization as far as a career was concerned.

"Tell you what," the admiral said, looking straight at the young pilot, those bushy eyebrows almost like exclamation points, "I think you should stay in. If you do, and if you ever feel you're being discriminated against because you're an ex-reserve, you call me on the telephone, and we'll talk about it."

Hank Suerstedt did stay in the Navy, in a few months becoming a "regular" officer, and never did have cause to telephone Bull Halsey. He couldn't know it on that fateful evening of 1945, but his career, during which he was destined to achieve flag rank, was to be closely allied with the AD Skyraider. In fact, the airplane was to become a major part of his professional life.

Suerstedt had felt the call to the skies before joining the Navy and earned a commercial license while attending San Francisco City College. He enlisted in February 1941 under the V-5 aviation cadet program. By late 1941 he had earned his gold wings and was a twenty-one-year-old ensign.

After a duty tour as a flight instructor he joined Composite Squadron 21 (VC-21) and the USS *Marcus Island* (CVE-77) in 1943. By 1945 he was a lieutenant commander and skipper of Torpedo Squadron 100, flying Avengers. Before war's end he had 160 combat missions under his belt. Later he commanded Escort Carrier Air Group 84 and from 1948 to 1949 was commanding officer of VA-213, a night, all-weather unit that also flew TBMs.

A few days after the Korean War began, he was assigned to BuAer in Washington, D.C. as AD class desk and project officer. In the years to come he would be the first skipper of the USS *Tripoli*, LPH-10, and deputy commander of the U.S. Naval Forces Vietnam as well as the commander of CTG 194.7, the "Brown Water Navy," the same as Paul Gray. He had this last assignment in 1970 and later commanded the Naval Weapons Center, China Lake, California.

Through his career, Suerstedt had a penchant for learning how to do things better. He was a thinking man's aviator.

"During the war in the Pacific," he said, "we flew low on missions and were often exposed to enemy fire during attack runs or while searching for targets. Our radar altimeters were so unreliable that the only safe way to fly low at night was to drop down until we saw our exhaust flames' reflection on the water, then judge our altitude by the intensity of the reflection."

He continued, "I lacked seniority to lead large, on-call, land target strikes or close air support missions on land targets. At the same time I was too senior to feel fully useful as a follower or as a bomb carrier on these strikes. I felt far more fulfilled doing target observation or target identification flights. There, flying alone at low altitudes, we were often exposed to and hit by small-arms fire. On two occasions my crewmen were wounded. One was a Marine Corps artillery observer struck in the shoulder. The aircraft were occasionally also damaged in critical sections, but we made it back to the carrier all right. It would have been more comforting, however, without the holes.

"The only armor on the TBM was a sheet of iron under the radioman in the lower radio compartment, and a small plate at the bottom of the ball turret. In the interest of future progeny I desired some protection under the pilot's seat also, as well as some safeguards for all of us around the sides of the fuselage. In both instances mentioned above, fuselage armor probably would have prevented the crewmen's wounds. It would cost some weight and a slight degradation of aircraft performance. But in the future it might save lives. Accordingly, with some assistance, I worked up a plan to attach armor to the TBM for future air observer missions in the Pacific and sent the plan through channels."

Nothing came of his proposal at the time, but the idea stayed with him, to reemerge when he had the BuAer job in Washington. It was especially on his mind when he reviewed combat reports, which he had access to on a regular basis. Obviously the Navy was losing Skyraiders to ground fire at a fearful rate.

In their courageous zeal to hit the enemy hard and often, Navy and Marine Corps pilots, especially those flying the ADs, were wreaking havoc on the Communist foe. By pressing their attack to low altitudes, à la Paul Gray, they were achieving devastating accuracy. But they were paying a price for it. They were incurring battle damage that even the sturdy and resilient Able Dog could not altogether withstand. Thus, a number of planes were knocked from the sky. Significantly, many were disabled by shrapnel from their own bomb blasts. Pilots would swoop in low, release their bombs, and pull sharply up and away, but fail to escape the fragmentation pattern of shrapnel from the exploding weapon because of their proximity to the ground. Yet on highway and rail cuts it was almost mandatory to carry attacks down to the "deck" to score good hits.

"At one point in the autumn of 1950 we believed we were going to run out of ADs," recalled Suerstedt. "We projected that within nine months to a year at the existing attrition rate, the Skyraiders would be nearly gone."

The first AD-5 flew in August 1951 but did not fight in Korea. Some called it the best Able Dog of all because of its versatility. This one was photographed in July 1953.

Fewer than a thousand of the attack bombers had been delivered since the assembly line began to roll in 1945. With the growing presence of jet airplanes, the days of the prop-driven ADs seemed to be numbered, whatever happened in Korea. While the AD-4N version was still in production in 1950, the "straight" AD-4 line was scheduled to close in fiscal year 1951. (Through the years, the Skyraider assembly line actually was stopped three times before starting up again. Heinemann and the Douglas Company didn't break up the tooling after each stoppage, demonstrating excellent foresight. This enabled the Skyraider to go back into production with minimum delay when new orders were received.)

Suerstedt contacted a Douglas Aircraft Company friend and associate, Bob Canaday, with whom he worked closely, their mutual interest being the AD. Canaday, a senior naval representative for Douglas in Washington, had literally grown up with the Skyraider. Together the naval officer and the company man coordinated efforts to make sure that more ADs were ordered. This collaboration of sorts, between a government contractor and a naval officer, would, in the end, be clearly justified.

"It was bold of me as a lieutenant commander, I suppose, but I wrote a letter and forwarded it up the channels to the chief of BuAer," said Suerstedt. "The gist of it was: 'In view of the hostilities and significantly high combat losses of ADs in Korea, I urge that immediate action be taken to initiate a new contract for additional AD aircraft.'

"My letter was returned bearing a cryptic note which was like a sock to the head: 'Zapateros A Tus Zapatos,' which is Spanish for 'Shoemaker, to your shoes.' The memo was signed by a senior plans officer and was his way of telling me to mind my own business.

"But I felt so strongly about keeping the Skyraider alive and minimizing losses," said Suerstedt, "that I was really stirred up now." (Indeed, Suerstedt even wrote to Arthur Godfrey, the famed entertainer, who had had some naval aviators on his radio program but who had failed, in Suerstedt's eyes, to properly extol the virtues of the Skyraider. "We believe," he wrote, "that like the Chesterfield Company, the Lipton Tea Company, National Hebrew Salami, and Mae West, if you've got something good you should let the public know about it!" He barraged Godfrey with a model of the AD complete with ordnance load and enough propaganda about the bird to occupy hours of air time.)

Said Suerstedt, "I asked Canaday for assistance, and Bob summoned help from his ordnance and engineering groups. They expeditiously produced a small replica of the AD featuring entry and exit holes that depicted typical damage patterns from anti-aircraft and small-arms fire. Douglas personnel had used battle damage reports to precisely locate common 'hit' areas. Lucite rods were placed through the in-and-out holes so that the model took on the likeness of a porcupine."

Meanwhile, some foreign technology specialists across the Potomac in the Pentagon (Suerstedt's office was in the Main Navy building) as a priority project had been studying the Stormovik, a World War II Russian attack plane that was heavily armored with steel boiler plate. They concluded that the Soviet design was much too heavy for the amount of protection it provided.

"Douglas came up with a design package whereby sections of armor plate made of steel and duraluminum (an alloy of aluminum, copper, manganese, magnesium, and silicon) in thickness from one-eighth to one-half inch could be strategically placed over the Skyraider's most vulnerable areas as revealed in the 'porcupine' model," said Suerstedt. "The sections weighed about 600 pounds, which was acceptable because they did not significantly degrade flying characteristics or performance. There would be only a 1.5-knot decrease in VMax, or maximum velocity.

Planes and plane sections equipped with armor plate were tested at Patuxent River, Maryland, Quonset Point, Rhode Island, and Dahlgren, Virginia. The tests showed that a .50-caliber bullet could penetrate plating that was a half-inch thick, but its velocity was so retarded that no significant damage occurred. A twenty-millimeter high-explosive incendiary shell "dished" and cracked the plate, but no fragments of the shell entered the aircraft.

One piece of half-inch-thick aluminum was rigged directly behind the pilot's seat to reduce the hazard of injury from a six o'clock hit. Others, a half-inch thick, protected the T-shaped area on the under fuselage beneath the cockpit wing stubs and fuel cell. More pieces were mounted around the engine and fuselage. Some especially vulnerable sections had steel plates inside the duraluminum, installed primarily to stop ball-type ammunition.

It wasn't easy procuring precious aluminum for his project. Even if Suerstedt's plans were sound, he had trouble getting the raw materials to implement them. Aluminum was in great commercial demand during the postwar boom. Truck trailer manufacturing companies as well as storm window manufacturers needed it in abundant quantities.

Suerstedt, however, lacked neither ingenuity nor guile. He put the arm on a friend and fellow naval aviator who flew ADs and who just happened to be serving as the naval staff member and special assistant for military production in the Office of the Secretary of Defense in Washington. Lieutenant Commander Williard "Willy" Nyburg was the man.

"I briefed Willy at a cocktail party," said Suerstedt. "'We need the aluminum badly,'" I told him. 'Otherwise we're going to end up with zero Skyraiders.'"

A spirited flyer and officer in his own right, Nyberg said, "Where do you want the stuff delivered?"

It wasn't quite that simple, of course, but a few weeks later the phone rang in Suerstedt's office. A senior Douglas man was calling from the plant in El Segundo. (The engineering people at Douglas had agreed to fabricate the plates for the aircraft, Suerstedt believed, on the assumption that it would take at least a couple of years to get the duraluminum for the AD.)

"I got eight box cars of aluminum sitting out here," he said increduously. "What do I do with the stuff?"

"Make armor plate," answered Suerstedt, with a deep sense of satisfaction.

He had pulled a coup. Less than a handful of people in the Navy Department knew how he got that aluminum, but there was a war on, the fighting was intensifying, and the "how" mattered less than the fact that it was on hand and ready for use by the Navy and Douglas.

"I waited a long time for the other shoe to drop," remembered Suerstedt. "I realized I might have signaled the end to my own Navy career by circumventing the system. I was also worried that even after all the effort, the armor plate wouldn't prove as valuable as I thought and that I had put Willy on the barbecue spit with me. It was a gamble but we believed in it."

As with any relatively new concept there was resistance to the use of armor plate. Not a few aviators felt it wasn't worth the expenditure. But Suerstedt pressed his case and even sought a somewhat devious assist from the U.S. Marine Corps.

Ken Reusser (produced ricer), a major in the BuAer armament section, had worked with Suerstedt all the way through the armor plate affair and was of great assistance in adding the two extra twenty-millimeter guns to the Skyraider (giving it four) some time earlier. (Interestingly, this same Marine Corps pilot was known as "Rice Paddy Reusser" because he had been shot down several times in Korea in Corsairs.)

With Reusser's wise help the message went out to the right people in Headquarters Marine Corps in Washington that the "Marine Corps was probably getting the shaft because AirLant and AirPac [Aviation staff personnel in the respective Atlantic and Pacific coasts] wanted it [the armor plate], and there had been no provisions made for outfitting the Marine ADs."

Within days after the first armor plate kits became available at El Segundo, supplies of them were loaded in Marine aircraft transports along with Douglas personnel field teams and flown to Korea for installation on the Navy's combat-exposed ADs.

And shortly after arousing the Marine Corps, Suerstedt told an AirPac representative that the "Marines are pulling one on the Navy by gathering up all the available armor plate for themselves. You better hustle to get your share."

This sort of scheming worked, and the demand for armor plate increased decisively. Suerstedt won his case, but, more important, as the plate went into combat in 1952, the loss rate of Skyraiders decreased significantly.

So, while the veracity of Suerstedt's remarks about Airlant and

Suerstedt's perseverance paid off. Tests depicted in this pictures led to installation of armor plate on front-line ADs. Shown is a section of aircraft before tests and a close-up of plating after being subjected to gunfire. (Suerstedt)

AirPac may not have withstood questioning, the ploy succeeded. As time went on, he effectively played various groups against each other for the benefit of all. Moreover, the armor plate boosted the flyers' morale in two important ways: there was the practical aspect, in the protection it provided; and there was the philosophical one—it demonstrated that some people back home were, indeed, looking after them.

When it came time to rotate from shore to sea duty Suerstedt had his choice of flying jet-powered F9F Panthers, Corsairs, or Skyraiders, as a squadron commanding officer.

"Since I'd been the AD class desk officer, I developed a paternal affinity for the plane. It seemed best to stay with what I knew," said Suerstedt. "Plus, I experienced a strong feeling of moral obligation to the aircraft."

He chose the Able Dog and in early 1953 became the skipper of VF-54, replacing the illustrious Paul Gray. Now thirty-two years old and still a lieutenant commander, Suerstedt had had an extraordinary amount of operational and command experience. Additionally, he had logged more than 3,000 hours in carrier aircraft, a figure well above the average.

One of the new C.O.'s cardinal rules in training was that pilots could go no lower than 3,000 feet on dive-bombing attacks. Thus, pilots made their pull-ups higher above the terrain with, initially, great anguish and emotion and some sacrifice in accuracy. But the higher altitude would make it tougher on the North Koreans to score hits and kept the Skyraiders out of the more lethal range of ground fire and their own bomb blasts. He was echoing the policy set forth by Admiral Soucek of Task Force 77 but on his own was totally convinced of its viability.

Eventually, before going into combat, the flyers fine-tuned their techniques and found they could achieve excellent accuracy with bombs. (During this training period Suerstedt also had his troops practice the Thach Weave, a tactical maneuver named after Admiral Jimmy Thach, who pioneered its development in World War II to combat the Japanese Zero, which had a performance edge at the time against U.S. naval aircraft. Although it was a fighter technique, Suerstedt had the foresight to envision a situation "where we might encounter Soviet jets." It didn't happen on his watch but he said, "We practiced against F2H Banshees and F9F Panthers. A couple of years later there did take place a dramatic confrontation involving ADs and Soviet-built prop fighters near Hong Kong"

Skyraider

(described later in this chapter). Skyraiders eventually took on MiGs in Vietnam, as chronicled in Chapter 6.

Once the pilots were in Korea on close air support and other special missions, the altitude restriction was lifted. The AD drivers were allowed to press their attacks down to very low altitudes if necessary. On one such strike in February 1953, in support of UN troops attempting to retake a ridge line, dug-in enemy troops and emplacements were hit with 1,000-pound bombs and other ordnance by Suerstedt's flyers within *seventy-five yards* of friendly front lines. While the ground fire threat, not to mention the danger from fragmentation patterns, increased under such circumstances, the risk was justified in light of the importance of protecting troops on the ground.

In the days before the AD-4 line was re-started in 1952, BuAer configured about eighty of the AD-4Ns (the night attack versions with two crewmen in the back) to AD-4NAs, supposedly with only a pilot. These were stripped of all their special night gear such as radar and certain electronic items. In the early -4NAs the two crewmen seats from the -4Ns and simple communications equipment were put into special kits and kept in storage in facilities on the West Coast. Before deploying, VF-54 was assigned ten AD-4NAs, into which six of the kits were placed, thus allowing Suerstedt's squadron, unlike other single-place, day attack units, space and seats in which to carry their coffee mess, key maintenance personnel, plane captains, and other high-priority cargo. They became a kind of sophisticated U-Haul vehicle.

"Both the AD-4 and -4NA," said Suerstedt, "were faster than the Corsairs which also flew with us aboard the USS *Valley Forge* [VF-54's new ship]. When coming off a target with our bombs gone, we actually had to throttle back a little so that the Corsairs could maintain their fighter cover for us. Also, we always tried to have a couple of -4NAs with seats in the back on each mission to serve as flak suppressors." (The -4NAs were very effective in this role because of their ordnance-carrying capacity compared to the Corsair and the Panthers.)

Also, having AD-4NAs with seats on a flight allowed the squadron to fly to airfields in South Korea, including Yodo Island, a United Nations–manned post in the middle of Wonsan Harbor, where they could collect pilots taken there after being shot down. The island featured a 200-foot-wide, 2,400-foot-long airstrip used primarily for emergency landings. Naval and Marine personnel operated the island station, the highest point of which was 377 feet, excellent for observing activities in the harbor.

Said Suerstedt, "If we didn't get pilots back shortly after they were downed, they were placed into a lengthy retrieval system that sent them back to Seoul for two weeks of debriefing by an Escape and Evasion Center. They would eventually return to us by TBM CODs [carrier on-board delivery aircraft] which ferried aircrews and other personnel to the carriers. We needed the aviators on the line. If a pilot was unharmed and picked up shortly thereafter by a rescue helicopter, and brought to friendly forces, he had little to add to escape and evasion lore."

One of the most unheralded and magnificent achievements in the Korean War was the ability of enlisted maintenance personnel to keep the aircraft in the air.

"We had 93 percent availability in VF-54 for the whole deployment during which we flew 3,500 combat hours," said Suerstedt. "This allowed us also to expend almost 1,800 tons of ordnance. This was incredible. Our troops put in 18- and 20-hour days working on the birds. Guys would fall asleep under airplanes and have to be awakened and ordered to their bunks. Lieutenant (Junior Grade) Andy 'Ski' Szymanski, who also worked for Paul Gray, was a key member of the team. They were a spectacular group of men."

A night attack "team" from VC-35 was assigned to Suerstedt's squadron. The AD-4Ns they flew, unlike VF-54's stripped AD-4NAs, had a large radar, electronic equipment, and crewmen. Suerstedt believed the men of VC-35 were the world's best aviators because they routinely flew from the straight-deck carrier (as compared to the much safer angled-deck flattops of today) in the worst of winter weather.

"They would frequently catch freight trains between tunnels," said Suerstedt. "Using radar to acquire the target and flares to illuminate it, they would fly down valleys with high mountains on all sides and attack, being careful to avoid flight beneath the flares which would be like pointing an arrow at themselves for the benefit of the enemy. The worse the weather was, including ice and snow storms, the more trains they got. We tried accompanying them on occasion to augment their bomb loads but decided that even if such missions might have been successful, they were hairy as hell. The VC-35 people were trained for such labors. We were not. We got our trains in the daylight."

Hank Suerstedt rendezvoused with "his Coronado, California

Skyraider

across-the-street-neighbor" Captain Harold G. Bowen, at the Officer's Club in Yokosuka, Japan one evening in the winter of 1952–1953. Bowen was the commodore of a destroyer squadron, which like Suerstedt's carrier was taking a respite from combat. They got to talking about their roles in the fighting, and before their conversation concluded that night they had formulated a tactical strategy that was destined to reap dividends on the battlefront.

Their respective units had unlikely call signs. VF-54's was "War Cry." Bowen's collective call for his destroyer squadron was "Cocktail Love." Despite the disparate thoughts those titles insinuated, War Cry's ADs blended with Cocktail Love's guns in a two-punch coordinated effort that really worked. The arrangement wasn't exactly sanctioned by higher authority, but what the two officers contrived really made sense.

"Some of our AD missions in North Korea at the time were known as 'Cherokee strikes,'" said Suerstedt. "On these routine air strikes we frequently bombed not always distinguishable lumps under the snow which purportedly were enemy supply stacks. These targets, which each pilot had noted on a photograph, were marked by a photo interpreter with black ink checks. Usually, they were located by grid coordinates annotated on the photos. The most rewarding thing about these strikes was finishing them without anyone being shot down or 'shot up.' We then sometimes were able to allow time following the 'Cherokee' to rendezvous with Hal Bowen's destroyers at Wonsan Harbor.

Using a personal code, Hal and I traded mesages explaining where we would be and when we would be there. One or more of Bowen's destroyers would approach the beach and begin probing the cave type storage areas along the shore with their guns. We'd then position our ADs behind the coastal mountains, out of sight, but in radio contact with Cocktail Love.

"The destroyer served as a teaser. Its goal was to 'smoke out' and draw fire from the communist batteries concealed in the mountain recesses. We would then mutually spot the enemy fire and pounce on its source with our bombs. We did have to do a little extracurricular activity on the flight deck before we launched, however.

"The CAG ordnance officer customarily went through our flock of ADs before takeoff, checking that the fusing on our bombs was correct. Usually, for Cherokee targets, a VT, proximity, or contact setting was in order because of the frozen ground. However, after he was gone we would, somewhat furtively I admit, reset the fuses on two of the larger bombs for detonation with a .002 second delay.

The USS *Princeton*'s VA-195 earned notoriety when a kitchen sink was attached to a 2,000 pounder and dropped on a North Korean target.

This allowed us to do more damage to the caves and guns, assuming we made good hits, of course."

This airdale–black shoe endeavor worked for some time. War Cry and Cocktail Love enjoyed a rewarding experience. For the Reds, the collaboration was a headache. Bowen, incidentally, reached flag rank and retired as a Vice Admiral.

One day a fleet commander observed a VF-54 AD-4NA pick up a rescued pilot at the Yodo Island way station. The flag officer walked over and inspected the aircraft. The admiral was inspired that night to request two AD-4NAs for a special mission the following day.

"I suspected that the 'mission' involved transporting the officer and and his guests to a South Korean Island where the hunting was exceptionally good," said Suerstedt. "I learned I was right later on."

Despite complaints to the Carrier Division staff, the planes were listed on the flight schedule. That night, as a means of mild protest, the squadron's painters took brushes in hand and created a logo on the outside of the two aircrafts' passenger doors. It consisted of the squadron insignia and the following: VR (the "R" stood for trans-

Skyraider

port under the Navy's designation system) 54 SCROD AIRLINES. (In fishing lore, a scrod is a young cod.)

This was a play on the acronym "COD" for carrier onboard delivery. The two pilots scheduled to fly the VIP hops next day, when asked to explain the terminology, were instructed to tell this story:

"Two women used to ride the same train to Boston every Friday. One asked the other, 'Why do you go to Boston?' 'To get scrod.' answered the woman. 'So do I' said the first, 'but I never used that tense of the word to describe it.'"

The plane painters also created a sign for passengers over the rear door that could be seen as they exited the aircraft. It read: "You have just been SCROD."

The pilots reported that all riders laughed about the name, and after that, the few times the AD-4NAs were requested by the fleet commander, the message always asked for "Two of VF-54's SCROD aircraft."

There was need for humor in those grim days. Casualties on the ground and in the air were heavy. There was a feeling among those doing the fighting that they were putting their lives on the line in a forgotten war, that the American people didn't care what was happening in a place far, far away from friendly shores.

As far as the Joint Chiefs of Staff were concerned, Korea was considered a peripheral theater. Their principal focus was on the Soviet threat to Europe. General Omar Bradley, chairman of the Joint Chiefs of Staff, later said in reference to the Korean conflict that it was "the wrong war, at the wrong place, at the wrong time, and with the wrong enemy." Whatever the philosophical implications of such thoughts were, Suerstedt's squadron lost six airplanes. Five of the pilots were saved; the other was killed.

Said Suerstedt, "The Skyraider lived up to its expectations in Korea, and that's about the best thing that can be said about a flying machine built for warfare." The AD was destined to prove that axiom again and again in the years ahead.

In any case, on 27 July 1953 a cease-fire was signed ending the thirty-seven-month war. In their book, *The Sea War in Korea*, Malcolm W. Cagle, who retired as a vice admiral, and Frank A. Manson wrote that "the AD Skyraider was the most successful aircraft of the 37-month war. Only the Skyraider could carry and successfully deliver the 2,000 pound bomb with dive bombing precision against the targets of interdiction; the bridge abutment or span, the tunnel mouth, and the cave entrance. The AD's versatility and weight-lifting capacity [as much as 5,000 pounds on an average carrier mission] made it the war's outstanding performer."

Juan Santos, Jr., an aviation buff whose father helped maintain Marine Corps Skyraiders in Korea, put it this way: "The AD was our tank in the sky."

Although Korean hostilities had ended, tranquility was still a dream in the far Pacific. In May 1954 French-held Dien Bien Phu, North Vietnam, fell to the Communists, led by Ho Chi Minh. Mainland China had exchanged gunfire with Formosa over custody of Quemoy and Matsu islands. Physician Dr. Tom Dooley, formerly of the U.S. Navy, was working wonders, peaceably, among the people of Indochina. But the seeds of turmoil had long since been sown and were destined to overwhelm hopes of stabilizing the part of the world that lay along China's southern flank. Carriers and other ships of the American fleet continued, therefore, to maintain a presence in the Pacific.

On 23 July 1954, about a year after the cease-fire was signed at Panmunjom, Korea, a Cathay Pacific Airways DC-4 en route to Hong Kong was shot down by Chinese Communist aircraft off the coast of Hainan, a large Chinese island southeast of Haiphong and southwest of Hong Kong. Reports indicated that two fighters attacked the helpless transport, knocked one of its engines out, and repeatedly strafed the aircraft as it descended and struck the water. Although nine people survived the crash, ten, including three Americans, perished. International tensions were heightened, and within a few days AD Skyraiders would become embroiled, if only briefly, in the aftermath of the tragedy.

The USS *Philippine Sea* with Carrier Air Group Five aboard, was deployed in the Pacific at the time. Its complement of aircraft included a fighter squadron sporting new F9F-6, swept-wing Cougar jets. "Defenders of the Fleet," they were called. A photo-reconnaissance detachment also had Cougars, while two other fighter squadrons operated the older Panthers. VC-3 was aboard with F4U Corsair night fighters. VC-11 had AD-4W Guppies, and a team from VC-35 flew AD-4Ns. VF-54, now commanded by Commander Christian Fink, piloted AD-4s and, of course, its SCROD "airliners."

Lieutenant (Junior Grade) John Rochford, who flew on Hank Suerstedt's wing in Korea, remembered those days in the summer of 1954. Said Rochford, "It was terribly hot. The carriers didn't have much air conditioning then, and people slept on catwalks, the flight deck, any cool spot they could find. We didn't fly as much as we'd like because operating funds were in short supply. We'd be at sea one week but fly only one day during that time. Then we'd go into port.

"When we had liberty in the Philippines there sometimes were three carriers in Manila Bay at the same time," recalled Rochford. "Having boat officer duty was an experience. LCUs [landing craft utility boats] were used to transport liberty parties to Sangley Point, a long 45 minutes away, and to Manila, also a 45-minute ride. Late at night those returning liberty boats were filled with happy crewmen from three different carriers. Keeping matters under control wasn't always easy.

"Finally, we went to sea for several days of flying, a great event for us even though we were instructed to remain 50 miles from any land. On the fourth day we manned up but were recalled to the ready room. 'Well,' we figured, 'we should have known it was too good to be true. We're not gonna fly today after all.' Instead, we learned that the Cathay Airliner had been shot down. We were ordered to search for survivors along the Hainan coast, staying 13 miles off shore."

Continued Rochford, "The Chinese claimed a 12-mile territorial limit although the U.S. believed a three-mile limit was proper. Anyway, 16 ADs took to the air and began the patrol. I spotted a Royal Navy flying boat that day plus a U.S. Air Force amphibian which had bravely landed and rescued nine survivors of the crash who were in a raft and later gave an account of the unprovoked attack. Back aboard our carrier we learned we'd be armed for subsequent search missions. The Cougars, by the way, were having a high time intercepting Pan American Airliners and waving at the stewardesses who waved back. We kidded them about wearing their tiger ties and defending the fleet.

"I had duty on the 25th and didn't fly. But next day, I went out on the 0900 launch. It was to be a flight I'd never forget. We formed a stair-step type formation with four ADs at 500 feet, four at 3,000 feet, and four more at 5,000. Each division was in tactical formation, the first section of two aircraft offset, or 'spread,' from the second so that each element could 'cover' the other's tail and maneuver accordingly, making turns or scissoring (reversing) into each other as necessary. Two Corsairs were at 10,000 feet while about five miles in trail from the main formation was an AD-4W Guppy serving as a communications relay with the ship. Two AD-4Ns were in company with and protecting the Guppy."

Key players in this flight were Lieutenant Commander Paul Wahlstrom, VF-54's executive officer, leading the first division at 500 feet, with Lieutenant (Junior Grade) Dick Ribble on his wing and Lieutenant (Junior Grade) John Damian and Ensign John Zardus in the second section. At 3,000 feet were Lieutenant Commander Bill Alexander, Lieutenant (Junior Grade) Ted Korsgren, Rochford, as second section leader, and Ensign Dick Crooks on his wing. The CAG, Commander George Duncan, had the 5,000-foot division with Ensign Dick Neubauer and Lieutenant Roy "Toot" Tatham. Toot was the second section leader and didn't have a wingman because the latter's Skyraider went down on the flight deck with a bad magneto check.

In the Corsairs were Lieutenant Commander Bud Salsig and Ensign E. L. Sutherland. Lieutenant Pete Choreff was in the Guppy with aircrewmen AT3 R. W. Baker and ATAN C. J. Blum. Escorting them were Lieutenant Max Puckett with ATAN R. G. Buckingham and Airman N. S. Osburn in one AD-4N, and Lieutenant W. P. "Robbie" Robinson, AD3 W. G. Cridland, and Airman B. C. Brand in the other.

The flight proceeded along the coastal area southeast of Hainan working its way up the eastern edge of the island carefully maintaining the twelve-mile distance and scanning the water below for any sign of life. Near the northern limit of their track two northeast-bound freighters and a smaller vessel ahead of them were spotted. Seaward from them, also on a northeasterly course, was a pair of U.S. destroyers. There were also many sampans in the area.

Wahlstrom, at the lowest level of the group, was in charge of navigation, and at the reversal point of the search track radioed that he was commencing a 180-degree turn. His two sections began executing a turn into each other, at the completion of which they would be aligned as they were when northbound. The other divisons would do the same.

"We were stacked in such a manner that you could look down and forward at the division below you," said Rochford. "As the first division passed below in its turn, the second was to begin its reversal. Toot Tatham, in CAG's division at 5,000 feet, had been a gunnery flight instructor with many hours towing a target sleeve and observing students making runs on the banner. He knew well when a pilot was too flat or too steep in a run. This turned out to be a big help to us."

Continued Rochford, "As Wahlstrom's division entered the turn, Toot saw two aircraft above him to his right. Initially, he thought they might be Max and Robbie having gotten ahead of the Guppy.

He kept looking and realized the planes were not ADs. Suddenly, these two 'strangers' began making a run that resembled those of his gunnery students. 'Bogies at four o'clock high,' he called, 'and they're making a gunnery run.' Four o'clock high didn't mean much to Wahlstrom's flight, which was half way into its turn. But the bogies kept coming and CAG, Neubauer, and Toot broke right. The attackers winged by, firing their guns at Toot first, then at CAG and Neubauer.

"Toot smartly reversed and got behind the bogies," said Rochford. "CAG transmitted, 'They're firing, they're firing. Shoot 'em down.' By now the division above us (CAG's) had moved off to my division's left side and my division leader was to my left. We broke to the left and started climbing. Tatham was on the tail of the first bogie and got a good shot at him. Meanwhile the second bogie was in a run. [The bogies were single-engine, propeller driven fighter-type planes. They had rounded wing tips and an air scoop beneath the fuselage, were greenish-brown in color, and had a broad white band around the outboard section of each wing. There was a red circle inboard on the top and another on the underside of the wings. The aircraft were later determined to be Soviet-built Lavochkin LA-7s which resembled American P-51 Mustang fighters. The pilots were presumed to be Chinese.] After the first whizzed by, my wingman somehow got on his tail and fired some 20-millimeter at him. Disabled, obviously hit by the cannons, the aircraft plunged straight into the water."

Alexander, Rochford's division leader, was in an extremely tight left turn as the second bogie fired at him. Rochford ended up on the tail of the second bogie at 3,000 feet. "He continued downward," remembered Rochford, "in a left, 360-degree turn. As I was adjusting my run, CAG was calling 'Shoot, shoot, shoot!' I pulled the trigger immediately. In the excitement I had forgotten to arm the guns. [The guns had an arm-safe switch. Circuit breakers for them were also customarily pulled when not in use to prevent mishap with the bolt mechanism during the charging sequence.] I frantically pushed the correct buttons and got one inboard and one outboard gun to fire. I recycled the arm-safe switch hoping to get the other cannons on the line, all the while tracking the bogie as he continued his 360-degree descending turn. We eventually rolled out at about 800 feet, still losing altitude.

"At this point I was out of ammo and quite disgusted that this guy hadn't gone up in smoke yet. In my frustration I was tempted to run up on him and chop off his tail with my prop. I moved up and to the right of the bogie, who was still descending, and could almost see the pilot in the cockpit. It's fortunate that I shifted position when I did because here came four Skyraiders swooping toward the bogie, firing away, followed by the Corsairs, who had come down from 10,000 feet and got off 50 or so rounds. Shortly thereafter the bogie crashed into the water."

Not surprisingly the formation was scattered about the sky, and CAG, wisely concerned about other bogies, ordered his aircraft to re-form. The smaller ship that was in front of the two freighters spotted earlier, was apparently a gunboat because it began firing on the U.S. planes. Commander Duncan requested permission from the *Philippine Sea* to attack this gunboat but was directed not to do so. The search for survivors was continued on the return leg as the pumped-up flyers relished their victory. They landed before noon after two and a half unforgettable hours in the sky.

Commented Rochford, "For a time we wondered if we'd have to face an international court. We all made detailed statements, and the communications center sent many a message that day. We received 'Well done's' and were very pleased with our accomplishment. That evening, Commander Fink, our C.O., placed a sign in the wardroom. It read: 'The C.O. of VF-51 [the Cougar squadron] will relinquish his tiger ties to the C.O. of VF-54, Defenders of the Fleet!' That generated a temporary bit of hate and discontent, but it was worth it.

"In retrospect," said Rochford, who continued his career as a naval aviator and retired as a commander with a great deal of Spad time in his log book, "the AD proved it was a formidable fighter in the low-altitude spectrum. Perhaps we didn't do as good a job as we should have, but under the circumstances it was still a successful flight. Toot and Dick Crooks, my wingman, were credited with downing the first LA-7. I shared in the kill of the second with Damian, Ribble, Wahlstrom, and Salsig, in his F4U.

"Interestingly, at the Navy Post Graduate school in Monterey, Calif., in 1966, I was studying international law. The 'Hainan Turkey Shoot,' it turns out, helped establish a principle that if fired upon on the high seas, you have the right to engage in hot pursuit even if the attackers return to their own territory. In our case we didn't have to do that since we were beyond the 12-mile limit throughout."

Concluded CAG Duncan in his report, "The overall pilot–aircraft performance of the enemy was inferior to that of the Navy Skyraiders. The enemy made ineffectual use of their altitude advantage and

Skyraider

in most cases the ADs turned inside of the attacking aircraft. I am proud to state that although the pilots who participated in this fight are not familiar with air to air combat, they joined the battle without hesitation, demonstrating a willing aggressiveness equal to the most experienced fighter pilots."

Key Skyraider men gathered here beside an A-4 Skyhawk in the late 1970s are Douglas Aircraft's Bob Canaday, R. G. Smith, Leo Devlin, and Ed Heinemann. Canaday was Douglas's Washington, D.C. representative; Smith, a configuration engineer and renowned artist; Devlin, Heinemann's right-hand man. (McDonnell-Douglas)

The Skyraider was powerful enough to be catapulted with the carrier at anchor. Here, AD launches while the USS *Hornet* is tied to Pier 12, Yokosuka, Japan, 1954.

Small in size but rich in talent was the U.S. Navy's Naval Air Maintenance Training Unit at Bien Hoa. (Moranville)

Rear Admiral Moranville, 1981.

Air Force Captain Bill Nicholson, in white suit, with Moranville next to him, socializes in Saigon, 1960. (Moranville)

Skyraiders operated aboard the USS *Bon Homme Richard* in Korea. Here, catapult officer on the same carrier in 1967 launches an A-1 on a combat mission in Vietnam.

South Vietnamese–piloted A-1Es pickle off napalm containers that explode, spreading jellied flame across the terrain.

As in Korea and World War II, enlisted men provided the muscle and maintainance ▶
skills in Vietnam. Without their efforts the Skyraider would never have achieved
such a successful and long life. Here, sailors from the *Intrepid* load a 2,000 pounder
on A-1 pylon in May 1966.

Number 577, one of the VA-25 A-1s involved in the MiG shootdown.

Number 572 was on the MiG shoot-down flight.

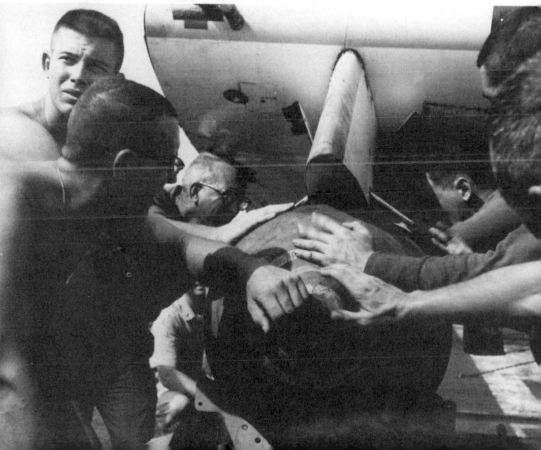

VA-25 Spads were based on the USS *Midway* in 1965. Four of them fly in echelon on practice flight when squadron was temporarily home-ported in Japan. (Bob Lawson)

Daramus with arm around fellow Fist of the Fleet pilot, Fred Freckman wearing Mae West. (Daramus)

A bar inserted into bombs before fuzing helped in the back-straining efforts to hoist the weapons up to the Spad's wing racks.

The USS *Hancock* in South
China Sea, 1966. Skyraiders
occupy stern. F-8 Crusaders
and A-4 Skyhawks are aligned
along edges of angled deck.

Mighty Mouse 2.75-inch rockets could be carried in nineteen-chamber pods.

116

Crew readies catapult on the *Coral Sea* as A-1 stands by.
▼

ring Yankee Station operations, final checker emerges from beneath bomb-laden Skyraider.
other catapult crewman signals pilot that tension is being applied to aircraft.

A-152 Skyraider is fired off on combat mission.

◀ Plane captains drag electrical starting cable out to VA-176 Spad on deck of the *Intrepid*, September 1966.

▶

This A-1 from VA-176 made it back to the *Intrepid* despite rudder damaged by ground fire on 1966 mission.

EA-1E approaches ship for landing after an electronic countermeasures mission.
▼

Head-on view of A-1E snagging a wire.

The Special Operations Squadron was still active in 1972 when this A-1 was photographed. Unit was then based at the Royal Thailand Air Force Base, Nakhon Phanom, Thailand.

Picture taken from A-1 cockpit shows 20-millimeter cannon on port wing paralleled by "daisy cutter" extensions which were inserted in nose of bombs causing them to explode just prior to weapons' actual impact with the ground. Smoke on ground is from previous bomb impacts.

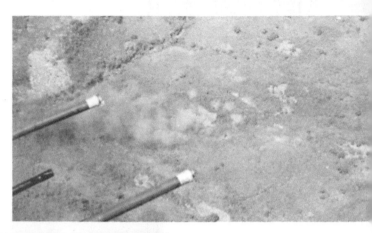

A-1E flown by U.S. Air Force wings over South Vietnamese jungle in 1966.

Prop of USMC AD-5 forms vapor trails on takeoff from the USS *Boxer* in 1955. This version of the Skyraider could be adapted to many missions, among them: day and night attack, passenger or troop carrier, ambulance, early warning, anti-submarine warfare, electronic countermeasures, target towing, and photo reconnaissance.

A Skyraider from the *Kitty Hawk* takes the cut in the early 1960s.

Skipper of VA-42, Commander I. W. Squire, makes the first AD landing aboard the USS *Forrestal* in January 1956, while airship observes.

Skyraiders as seen from directly overhead.

Author in VA-85 Skyraider refuels Royal Navy Scimitar during joint exercises in the Mediterranean in early 1960s.

Admiral Thomas H. Moorer, former chief of naval operations and chairman of the Joint Chiefs of Staff, was a captain when he and Ed Heinemann helped develop in-flight refueling capability for A-4 Skyhawk and other aircraft. The admiral said that "In some cases [the detachable external refueling system] was even better or more effective on the A-1 since the Skyraider it seemed had almost unlimited load capacity." An F3H Demon "gets a drink" from a Skyraider in 1957. An F4D Skyray plugs into "basket" of extended refueling line of VA-65 AD-6 in 1960. F-8 photo Crusader looks on.

Jets follow a prop. Cocked up in order to stay with the slower Skyraider are an F-8 photo Crusader and two other aircraft designed by Ed Heinemann and his Douglas El Segundo team: an A-3 Skywarrior, number 601, and an A-4 Skyhawk, number 306. All planes were from the *Forrestal*-based CAG-8 in early 1960s.

VAW-12 Guppy launches from the USS *Lake Champlain*.

5

A Nebraskan in Asia

And when the ordnance was gone, I flew a loop to a landing, taxied up to the line of VIPs almost like an ice-skater skidding to a stop, shut down the engines and jumped out of the cockpit, all smiles.

—Navy pilot in Vietnam, 1960

In the late 1950s, on the southeastern flank of the Asian continent about 2,000 miles below Korea, the South Vietnamese were engaged in a conflict with Communist-supported Viet Cong insurgents. The beleagured Republic of Vietnam (South Vietnam) had asked for U.S. assistance to augment the F8F Bearcats that their diminutive air force was flying. Hank Suerstedt, who was Asian training officer on the staff of CinCPac (Commander in Chief Pacific) got wind of the fact that the U.S. Air Force was scheduled to supply the South Vietnamese with F-80s. He contacted his old friend Bob Canaday and asked him the current location of ADs throughout the world, including those in storage at Litchfield Park in Arizona. He briefed CinCPac, Admiral Harry Donald "Don" Felt, who agreed that the Skyraider was much better suited for the mission at hand than were the Air Force jets.

Since the mid-1950s there had been strong advocates within naval aviation for "all-jet" air groups. Not a few people, especially those tasked with actual flight deck operations, believed their jobs would be much easier without a mix of props and jets. Still, as advanced as jets were in comparison with ADs, the piston-powered attack bombers simply could not be written off. They were still functioning as integral elements in seagoing air wings. One writer

Moranville's labors in 1960 helped lay the foundation for tactics used by South Vietnamese pilots later on. Here, an A-1E of the South Vietnamese Air Force makes a diving attack on a Vietcong target.

of the time called the Skyraider the "ultimate in aeronautical virtuosity." Admiral Felt did not disagree.

"By God," he told Captain Suerstedt, "we're gonna put ADs in there [Vietnam]."

Suerstedt suggested that the Southeast Asia Treaty Organization send fifty of the Douglas planes to Vietnam. He also proposed that they be flown by aviators "on leave" from the U.S. Navy under an AVG—Allied Volunteer Group—arrangement, à la General Chenault's Flying Tigers in World War II in China. Although that idea never materialized, about fifty Vietnamese pilots came to Texas and trained in the Skyraider at Naval Air Station Corpus Christi.

If there were a hall of fame for Skyraider pilots, one of the foremost candidates for induction would be a native of Guide Rock, Nebraska. He was a twenty-eight-year-old lieutenant when he became what could be described as the first operational U.S. naval pilot in Vietnam (i.e., the Vietnam War of the 1960s and 1970s).

It was 1960, long before the war in Southeast Asia blazed across international headlines. The Republic of Vietnam with Ngo Dinh Diem as president had been established following the fall of the French at Dien Bien Phu in 1954. Cease-fire agreements partitioned the country, separating the Communist north from the anti-Communist south at the 17th parallel. The last of the French troops left the country in 1956 while a small number of U.S. military advisors arrived to help train Diem's forces.

In bordering Laos the pro-Communist Pathet Lao were making a bid for power, and by the spring of 1959 their brothers in arms, the Vietcong (native guerrilla and combat groups of the National Liberation Front of Vietnam), were increasing their activity, supported and directed by comrades in the north.

The U.S. military advisory assistance group, called MAAG, was based in Saigon with a small contingent of mostly Army, Air Force, and naval personnel. There were about 700 Americans in the country at the time—civilians, military personnel, members of the diplomatic corps, and their dependents. The only U.S. naval aircraft was an aging C-47 flown by a lieutenant commander and a chief aviation pilot (an aviator who was a chief petty officer from the enlisted ranks) on routine logistic and transport missions.

Officials in the higher echelons of the American government wanted to help increase South Vietnam's effectiveness against the elusive Vietcong. Fighting was taking place across the face of the country, especially in the broad area ranging from the delta region below Saigon to Pleiku, about 250 miles north of the capital city. Although the combat encounters were on a smaller scale compared to what would occur in the years ahead, they were no less savage and intense.

The Vietnamese Air Force had one tactical unit, the First Fighter Squadron. Its pilots, who flew the F8F Bearcats, were based at Bien Hoa, a rather crude airfield about thirty miles north of Saigon, which had a 4,000-foot runway made of pierced steel planks and a few hangars and operations buildings, but neither navigational nor lighting aids. Thus Bien Hoa was a daytime, fair-weather airstrip.

The Grumman-built, propeller-driven fighters had been obtained from the French. Descendant of the F4F Wildcats and F6F Hellcats that had performed so well in World War II, the Bearcat had not been tested in combat. It arrived too late for World War II and was not used in Korea. But it was quite suitable for the Vietnamese, with two exceptions: it could not carry large ordnance loads, and replacement parts for it were nearly nonexistent. Also, having been designed for air-to-air combat, it could hardly be expected to excel in ground support or interdiction roles. Nevertheless, the courageous South Vietnamese pilots were using it effectively to strafe and bomb Vietcong troops in their jungle strongholds.

Meanwhile, Admiral Felt's efforts resulted in the decision to send twenty-five Skyraiders to Bien Hoa with one pilot to serve as a combination advisor and flight instructor. Six enlisted men were also assigned. They were to teach Vietnamese maintenance crews how the aircraft's systems worked.

Aviation Training Unit 301 was the training site for the Vietnamese. All U.S. naval and Marine Corps Skyraider pilots trained there before earning their wings and transferring to fleet squadrons. The unit enjoyed an extraordinarily high degree of morale. It had a corps of enthusiastic instructors and projected an almost palpable exuberance, which, more often than not, was characteristic of any outfit that flew the Skyraider.

The feeling around ATU-301 was that the Able Dog was a ticket to adventure. It was a spunky flying machine that spat in the eye of its polished, jet-propelled brothers. Rivalries between prop squadrons and those of the "tailpipe" set were in fun, of course. Yet the AD drivers deliberately fostered an image of themselves as a special breed; not necessarily a better breed, but at least one substantially different from the others.

It was no surprise that forty aviators, all from ATU-301, volunteered for the advisor/flight instructor job in Vietnam. And while it may have been disappointing to many, it was also no surprise that Lieutenant Ken Moranville, the Nebraskan, was tapped for the coveted assignment.

An aggressive pilot known as a demanding teacher in the air and a fierce competitor in athletics on the ground, he was considered a cut above his competent contemporaries.

Students tended to fear him. He had a reputation for being a perfectionist. But once they flew with him and realized how much they gained under his tutelage, the fear subsided and was replaced by an abiding respect. The author recalls a flight in 1959, for example, when he was a student at ATU-301.

An aviation cadet named Al Schilleci (Shi lay' see) was having difficulty learning dive-bombing techniques. Moranville was tasked with straightening him out. The author was assigned to ride with the instructor in the right seat of an AD-5 to serve as a recorder, taking notes.

Schilleci and three other students circled at 10,000 feet over the target, a series of 50-, 150-, and 300-foot concentric circles chalked in white on the arid ground, outlining a bull's-eye. Moranville orbited down low at 500 feet, clear of the firing line, continually maneuvering his aircraft for the best line-of-sight view of the plummeting ADs.

"If Schilleci can get an accurate picture of what a good run looks like coming down the 'chute' *and* score a good hit," Moranville said, "he'll be all right."

In the next half hour, the lieutenant demonstrated quintessential teaching ability. He literally "talk-flew" Schilleci's airplane for him. Somehow Moranville was able to project himself into the student's cockpit. He became Schilleci's eyes and limbs. Like a human computer he could quickly judge the distant aircraft's speed, altitude, roll-in point, and dive angle. He calculated the necessary corrections for wind direction and velocity. He issued concise and timely commands that Schilleci sharply obeyed.

"OK," Moranville began, as Schilleci banked toward an invisible reference point in the sky where his attack would begin. "Roll in now!"

High above, the Skyraider flipped on its back then reversed to an upright position, diving steeply. A second or two passed.

"Raise your nose five degrees," ordered the instructor, recognizing that Schilleci's dive was too steep.

Schilleci pulled back on the stick. His aircraft approached the proper "cone" over the target. "Now push it over," commanded the

Moranville poses with C.O. of the South Vietnamese fighter squadron he helped train. (Moranville)

instructor. "Dip your right wing . . . level your wings . . . stand by to release." The plunging Skyraider's line of attack shifted ever so slightly with the wing dip. "Pickle now!" directed Moranville.

The Mark 76 practice bomb, which resembled a real weapon in miniature but for its powder-blue color, sailed from its rack on the wing and struck the ground at the twelve o'clock position within 100 feet or so of the bull's-eye. A ten-gauge shot gun charge inside the bomb exploded, and a tiny white cloud rose from the scarred earth, signaling the hit. Meanwhile, Schilleci was pulling up and away, zoom-climbing to 10,000 feet for another run.

So it went. Schilleci continued to score well and eventually did get the picture. He was qualified and soon earned his golden wings. (It did not work against Schilleci that he was an excellent athlete and played with Moranville on the ATU-301 softball team.)

It would have been one thing for the lieutenant to achieve such effective instruction while riding directly behind a student in a tandem seat trainer with a view of the dive-bombing pattern identical to that of the cadet up front. But to accomplish it from a distance, almost by remote control, was another matter indeed.

In August 1960, after instructing six Vietnamese pilots in the Skyraider, Moranville left the sultry climate of southern Texas for a

Skyraider

similar environment in South Vietnam. He joined the four chief petty officers and two petty officers first class, each of whom was a well-versed technician and wrench-turner and especially proficient in maintaining the Skyraider. Although they were assigned administratively to the MAAG, Moranville and his team had little direct connection with the corps of Americans in Saigon. The enlisted men set up housekeeping in a barracks building, while Moranville lived in quarters that had previously accommodated the French officer who commanded the base when his country's regime was in power. The naval group worked and lived side by side with an Air Force contingent led by Captain Bill Nicholson, a veteran of aerial combat in Korea and the fighter advisor to the Vietnamese Bearcat pilots.

The first six (of twenty-five) Skyraiders, all AD-6s, arrived in early September by jeep carrier. The ship had steamed up the Saigon River to the city where the aircraft were offloaded and towed through the streets of Saigon and along a country road to Bien Hoa. Incidentally, Captain Hank Suerstedt was there to watch the birds arrive and to meet Ken Moranville.

U.S. Naval Ship *Core*, carrying A-1 Skyraiders, approaches berth in Saigon harbor in June 1965. A similar scene occurred five years earlier when Lieutenant Ken Moranville was an advisor to the South Vietnamese Air Force and a batch of attack bombers arrived.

The aircraft came without their normal seat parachutes. Moranville improvised and had his crew install back-pack type chutes that were available. This configuration was as unorthodox as it was uncomfortable for Moranville, but, ironically, it worked quite well for the smaller-sized Vietnamese. Coupled with built-up seat pans, the back-pack gave them closer access to the controls.

The small but talented maintenance team depreserved the birds, a laborious, time-consuming process that involved removal of protective coverings and fillers used to inhibit corrosion. Moranville was pleased with the overall condition of the aircraft, however.

"They were almost like new," he said. "They arrived directly from the rework facility at Naval Air Station Quonset Point, Rhode Island, where they were completely overhauled."

Moranville test-flew each of the machines as they became ready and quickly established a training syllabus for the Vietnamese. He "chased" them; that is, followed them closely as they checked out the new planes, flying either a Bearcat or a Skyraider, whichever was available. He soon had the Vietnamese handling the heavier and more powerful attack bomber with some expertise.

Ordnance was carried even on instructional flights to enhance realism. It also came in handy if a target suddenly became available. A typical ordnance load for the ADs included two napalm bombs, some 500-pound general-purpose bombs, and 2.75-inch, folding-fin rockets, normally carried in large cylindrical pods with nineteen chambers each. Although officially prohibited from direct combat action himself, Moranville was close enough to the action to see and feel it.

"The Vietnamese were flying 'on-call' strike missions," he recalled. "The VC (Vietcong) were terrorizing villages, quite often at night. Although we didn't fly after dark, the squadron launched at daylight to check out VC positions. L-19 spotter planes flown by Vietnamese were a big help. Generally, there was one division (four aircraft) airborne at all times during the day, while another division remained on an alert status adjacent to the runway. We had a superb security system, incidentally. Geese were strategically positioned by the airplanes and throughout the base. Especially effective at night, they really made a loud racket when anyone came near them.

"I remember demonstrating the AD's firepower before a group of military leaders one day not long after arriving at Bien Hoa. I carried a full load of rockets and bombs. I took off and made a few runs at a simulated target on the field. On one of the dives I simultaneously fired eight pods full of rockets, 152 in all. They really threw up the dust. And when the ordnance was gone I flew a loop to a landing, taxied up to the line of VIPs almost like an ice-skater skidding to a stop, shut down the engine, and jumped out of the cockpit, all smiles. I couldn't help showing off a bit and must admit I got a kick out of seeing the guests with their jaws agape in awe of the Skyraider's capabilities.

"In those days," said Moranville, "the war, for the most part, was a Monday-through-Friday, daylight-hours-only affair. That's hard to accept by many Americans. But the Vietnamese on both sides of the conflict had a different outlook of the combat situation. Their lives had been characterized and influenced by the miseries of fighting and violent death, literally from birth. There was no end of the turmoil in sight, either. War was all they knew. So, by a sort of unwritten agreement, Saturday and Sunday were off-days from the struggle. And during the week there was a definite relaxation of the fighting from one to three in the afternoon for a siesta. We tried once to establish a weekend alert force, but it didn't get much business."

That might explain why Moranville and Nicholson rose early on 11 November 1960, Armistice Day, a holiday, to go to Saigon to play some golf. The base commander at Bien Hoa, a Vietnamese major, spotted the pair, golf bags slung over their shoulders preparing to leave, and waved them back.

"There is a problem!" declared the major. "a coup against President Diem is taking place. The bridges to Saigon have been cut off."

Thoughts of golf instantly diminished. The two officers returned to their quarters, gathered up steel helmets, rifles, pistols, and ammunition, and proceeded to the operations area, where the enlisted men joined them for a tense vigil.

Unrest within Saigon government circles was not uncommon, but all hands were naturally concerned over who would emerge victorious in any political disturbance. The base commander was uncertain what parties were involved so urged the Americans to exercise caution.

"I was somewhat scared," said Moranville. "We were virtually cut off from MAAG headquarters and were really on our own."

The morning wore on uneventfully until about eleven o'clock when an L-19 motored in from the south like a lonely bird seeking refuge. The small spotter plane fluttered to a landing on the Marston matting of the parking area. Its pilot secured the engine switches and almost before the propeller quivered to a stop, hustled out of his machine. The major and the fighter squadron C.O. ran over to greet him, and there followed an animated exchange complete with wild arm motions.

The C.O. issued some abrupt commands, to which his pilots responded by scrambling to their planes, which were already fueled and armed. Six Skyraiders and a like number of Bearcats quickly belched smoke and rumbled to life. The planes methodically lumbered out to the approach end of the runway and roared in turn down the strip and into the sky.

The major hurriedly explained the situation to the Americans. A paratroop commander in Saigon had apparently launched a coup d'etat against President Diem.

"It appears that a company-sized column of troops is on the way to Bien Hoa," said the major with evident alarm.

Moranville's pulse quickened as the major tried to reassure the Americans.

"I will negotiate with them," he said, "so stand by and hope for the best."

The road leading to the main gate at Bien Hoa was two-laned and narrow; it could barely accommodate one car passing another. Moreover, it was banked about fifteen feet above the level of the rice paddies that flanked it. Moranville, Nicholson, and their men had taken position in the crude wooden tower atop one of the hangars. In the distance they could see the approaching truck column.

"Out front was a jeep with a machine gun mounted in the rear," said Moranville. "Directly behind it was a black Chevrolet sedan followed by many trucks."

Undaunted, the major marched beyond the perimeter of the base down the road toward the oncoming troops. He stopped after traveling about 50 yards, the gate directly behind him. The column also stopped, and a South Vietnamese general emerged from the sedan, waving his arms furiously.

"I didn't know what to think," said Moranville, "but I had to admire the major for confronting the general like that all by himself."

The general informed the major that he and his troops were going to take over the base and intended to isolate it completely until the coup played its course. He was, apparently, on the side of the paratroop commander. Meanwhile, the Bearcats and Skyraiders were getting airborne.

"The next thing we saw was the C.O. of the squadron in the lead Bearcat, bearing down toward the road at a 90-degree angle to it," said Moranville. "He was skimming just above the paddies, really whistling along, aligned with a point equidistant between the jeep at the head of the column and the gate. All eyes were trained on him."

The Bearcat was almost a blur as it neared the road. The C.O. pickled away a napalm bomb that soared from its rack and blasted into the earth, producing a searing wall of flame between the column and the gate. As the F8F banked away, a blazing, orange and black mass of fire was left in its wake.

Soldiers in the column scrambled recklessly from the trucks, most diving headlong into the rice paddies. Within minutes the roar of the Bearcat's engine served notice that the C.O. was making another run. He whizzed by a second time, on this occasion harmlessly, electing not to drop another weapon. The other Bearcats and Skyraiders joined in column and made repeated passes at very low level over the trucks.

Sensing that he was up against a superior force, the general decided to negotiate with the major. An intense conversation followed.

"Its hard to believe," said Moranville, "but in the moments that followed, those troops were literally 'herded' into a compound on the base by the Skyraiders and Bearcats circling overhead. Apparently, the sight of the heavily armed airplanes convinced the general to capitulate. I have to believe that that was the first, and probably only, time the Skyraider and the Bearcat were used like cowboys rounding up cattle into a corral.

"I learned later that Vietnamese Marines captured the rebel paratroopers on the grounds of the Palace in Saigon. They surrendered with their hands up. President Diem was subsequently freed and restored to power. The company at Bien Hoa was also liberated and no blood was spilled, at least at Bien Hoa. The Vietnamese Air Force remained neutral during the fracas." (President Diem remained in office, only to be assassinated three years later.)

Remembered Moranville: "On a training mission one day, an excited voice filled our earphones. I could usually sense when some heated action was taking place by the accelerated diction of the Vietnamese. In this case an L-19 pilot had spotted some Vietcong and dropped a signal-smoke grenade marking their location. The C.O. was in a Bearcat again and maneuvered into position for an attack with napalm. He rolled in and sped toward the smoke. He was so low he was almost brushing the tree tops. He pressed his release button and a napalm bomb fell away. A burst of jellied flame

The "1960" ADs were towed through Saigon as was this A-1E, wearing its preservative coating, in 1965.

saturated the pocket of jungle around the signal smoke, a perfect hit.

"No one's positive what went wrong, but the C.O.'s plane whipped into a roll out of control, almost simultaneously with the bomb impact, and crashed, killing him."

Some time later Vietnamese troops located and examined the wreckage. It appeared that one of the Bearcat's wings had been blown off in flight. "The baffling thing," said Moranville, "was that a bazooka was found in the path of undergrowth scorched by the napalm. We theorized that a Vietcong soldier—a mighty courageous one I might add—had stood up to the fighter and shot it down with that bazooka. To my knowledge that's the first and only time an aircraft may have been knocked out of the sky by such a weapon.

"Whether or not that was what happened, the upshot was that the crash had serious repercussions on the other flyers," Moranville added. "The Vietnamese were very superstitious about such things and no longer wanted to fly Bearcats in combat. The Skyraider therefore became their favorite plane."

Moranville left Vietnam at the end of 1960 but returned nine years later as executive officer of a carrier-based A-7 Corsair II squadron. He completed 110 combat missions in Southeast Asia.

"In 1969," he said, "as best as I could determine, only one of the 28 Vietnamese pilots I flew with was still alive. While I was at Bien Hoa, our only loss was the C.O. Those guys surely must have logged a lot of combat missions over the years."

While summarizing his 1960 experiences, Moranville recalled that he had the distinction of checking out General Nguyen Cao Ky, a transport squadron C.O. at the time, in an AD.

"He was flamboyant all right," said Moranville in reference to the man who became one of South Vietnam's most prominent leaders, catching the public's eye as a flashy figure in dark flight suit with his beautiful young wife at his side. "But he was also very competent. He was an excellent aviator. We knew back then that he was a 'comer.'"

Moranville also remembered the rudimentary approach procedures that were to be used in the event inclement weather forced either himself or Nicholson to return to Bien Hoa under instrument-flying conditions.

"Fortunately, we never had to use the procedure," he said, "but it was fun to practice it. We made an ADF (automatic direction finding) approach using the homer at Ton Son Nhut (the airfield in Saigon), lined up with the north runway there, and continued on over the city at 500 feet. Then we made a left turn at the Saigon River, following it until reaching the Bien Hoa River where we turned right. We passed *under* a bridge on the river then turned to zero three zero degrees for three miles. This fed us directly into Bien Hoa!"

He recalled another highlight: "I'll never forget a Sunday when I was supposed to play golf in Saigon. My tee-off time was 0900, but having had a bit too much to drink the night before, I overslept until 1100. Turns out I was very lucky. At precisely 0900 a bomb, presumably planted by a Vietcong, exploded in the wall of the men's locker room at the golf course, killing one person. I put away my golf bags for good—at least in Southeast Asia, after that."

No one relieved Moranville upon his departure from Bien Hoa. The advisory program continued in a modest way, however, until political events eventually led to the terrible holocaust that rocked the world for a decade.

At this writing in 1982, Bill Nicholson is a two-star general in the U.S. Air Force. Moranville became commanding officer of Naval Air

Station Cecil Field, Florida, where many of the U.S. Navy's east coast, carrier-based attack squadrons operate when not deployed aboard the flattops. He became a rear admiral in 1981 and was assigned as deputy chief of staff for Operations Command and Control for the commander in chief Atlantic Fleet. Nicholson and Moranville periodically get together for a game of golf at courses where the threat of unexpected explosions is minimal. Both remain fiercely loyal to the cause of the South Vietnamese and remain proud of their role in the abortive attempt to save that country from Communist domination.

"Despite the outcome of the war," said Admiral Moranville, "that period in 1960 in South Vietnam gave me the most exciting moments of my life. I can't say enough about the great airplane—the Skyraider—that I shared those moments with."

Unrest prevailed in Vietnam. After Diem's assassination in November 1963 (three weeks before President John F. Kennedy was killed in Texas), General Duong Van Minh took the reins of government. General Nguyen Khanh overthrew him in January 1964, and favored an invasion of North Vietnam. Meanwhile, the U.S. Navy patrolled the South China Sea not far from the Vietnamese coastline. Photo-reconnaissance missions were flown by carrier-based RF-8 Crusaders to monitor Communist activities. Then, in early August 1964, North Vietnamese torpedo boats made hostile runs on the destroyer USS *Maddox*. Counterattacks followed, and President Lyndon Johnson authorized an assault on major PT-boat installations located on the North Vietnamese coastline. All sides intensified build-ups of military forces. The war in Southeast Asia was soon in full swing, and naval task forces, spearheaded by carriers, were operating at combat tempo in the Gulf of Tonkin.

6

Skyraiders: 2, MiGs: 0

... the two tanks ... fell away. This sudden loss of weight and drag caused my Spad to actually leap upward, like a quickly rising elevator. At precisely that moment, bullets from the MiG zipped beneath me, their path through the sky signaled by tracer rounds, right where I was the instant before releasing the tanks.

> Lieutenant (Junior Grade) Charlie Hartman of VA-25 describing a portion of a Skyraider vs. MiG engagement in North Vietnam

It was Father's Day, 20 June 1965, a sultry summer Sunday on Yankee Station in the Gulf of Tonkin. A high overcast had turned the world at sea to gray. Over land, beneath the endless lid of clouds, visibility was excellent. The rich green forest and flat expanses of rice paddies of North Vietnam appeared tranquil despite the fact that the skies above them were a potential arena for combat.

An American F-105 pilot from the U.S. Air Force had been shot down by North Vietnamese ground fire in the vicinity of Dien Bien Phu. Although the USS *Midway* was on a "stand down," her duty rescap (rescue combat air patrol) was ordered into the air. Four A-1s from Attack Squadron 25 took off in midafternoon. Leading the flight was a veteran Skyraider pilot, Lieutenant Commander Ed Greathouse. His wingman was Lieutenant (Junior Grade) Jim Lynne, and in the second section were Lieutenant Clint Johnson and Lieutenant (Junior Grade) Charlie Hartman, the number three and four pilots. Although Greathouse was the most experienced of the group, all four flyers and their parent squadron had joined the fighting simultaneously and therefore had similar amounts of expo-

In hangar bay aboard the USS *Constellation*, mechanics C. E. Lewandowski and R. L. Sparr prepare to change the engine on this Skyraider.

Skyraider

sure to combat. Each of the Skyraiders carried a typical load for a search and rescue mission: four pods of 2.75-inch rockets and plenty of twenty-millimeter.

Greathouse led his flight over the beach at about 10,000 feet. They were below an overcast, which was at about 11,000 feet. Visibility was especially good below the clouds, which were stratus layers about a thousand to 1,500 feet thick. These clouds effectively cut out the sun. In another year or two, 10,000 feet would be an extremely precarious altitude because of the proliferating surface-to-air missile platforms in the north. In 1965, however, there were only a small number of Soviet-supplied SAMs in Vietnam. Anti-aircraft artillery was the major threat, and 10,000 feet was a reasonably safe altitude considering the enemy's known gun positions in the area.

As they proceeded inland, Greathouse signaled his wingmen to establish a combat spread formation, splitting into two sections, flying parallel, but with a half mile or so of distance between them. Each flyer thus had his own visual area of responsibility. With this lookout doctrine the formation was covered a full 360 degrees from attack. This flight disposition, incidentally, was a derivation of Jimmy Thach's weave, which influenced the training of Hank Suerstedt's and other attack type squadrons from the 1950s on. On this day in Vietnam the Thach philosophy would pay dividends, as it had done so often in the Pacific fighting in World War II.

A voice crackled in the earphones of the Skyraider pilots. It belonged to a radar controller on board a destroyer off the coast, assigned to monitor aerial activity.

"Canasta," the controller advised, referring to the VA-25 call sign. "There are bandits in the air." The A-1s were about fifty miles northwest of Thanh Hoa, a city about ninety miles south of Hanoi. The flyers continued on a northwest heading, wary now of this significant threat. The destroyer called again.

"The bandits are at your six o'clock, four miles," reported the controller. "There appear to be two of them, and the blips are merging together."

Said Hartman, "It was after that call that I looked behind us and saw them. As the number four man I was on Johnson's wing on the right flank of the formation. They were offset about one mile to our left flying straight and level at about 10,500 feet. I don't mind telling you my heart was really pumping. I was stunned. You don't see enemy fighters every day in your life. But there they were, a pair of silver machines, MiG-17s, heading roughly in the same direction we were."

"Clint [Johnson] was having radio trouble," he went on. "He probably knew what was happening but was unable to transmit." (He had actually experienced a radio failure.)

Remembered Ed Greathouse, "The MiGs were in right echelon. I believe they passed without seeing us. Jim Lynne and I spotted them at about our seven or eight o'clock and watched them continue on. Initially I thought they might be headed toward another flight of Spads from VA-196 which was operating in the area ahead of us. But when the MiGs were about one and a half, maybe two miles ahead, they executed a rapid reversal toward my section. My guess is they didn't spot us at first because we were just below the overcast and slightly down from them. Their radar operator on the ground probably realized the MiGs had overshot. Their reversal was very likely a response to a call from their controller. I transmitted a 'heads up' to the flight as they started the turn."

"The familiar story of the number four man being the first to get shot down on an initial attack raced through my mind," said Hartman, referring to tales of unseen fighters jumping a formation and knocking its trailing aircraft out of the sky first. In this case, however, once the MiGs turned, all the parties were in direct confrontation with each other. The melee was about to begin.

The closure speed between the combatants was nearly 600 knots. Action was imminent, as all six minds were working at breakneck speed framing thoughts and decisions that could spell the difference between triumph and disaster.

"Someone—I think it was Ed [Greathouse]—transmitted an expletive when he saw the MiGs bend around toward us," said Hartman. "What happened next was the correct, instinctive reaction on our part although the maneuver may not have been performed with precision. We split-S'ed and dove to the deck."

The opponents were now in a valley between two ridge lines about 1,500 to 2,000 feet high. The terrain was characterized by hills, some with sharply rising limestone peaks called karsts.

"We terminated the dive, leveled off, and flew at altitudes varying from 50 to 500 feet above the terrain," said Hartman, "following the southeasterly direction of a river." At this point, despite their being objects of a deadly pursuit, the Skyraiders were in their "own environment," hugging the ground. "We knew that the MiGs, just like most jets, would swallow more fuel in the denser air near the ground," said Hartman. "The enemy pilots had to be concerned with their increasing fuel consumption and, hopefully, this concern would serve to distract them. Anyway, one of the MiGs, who was a

R.G. Smith, instrumental in the design of the Skyraider, painted this view of North Vietnamese MiG-17, trailing flame and smoke, passing between Johnson and Hartman. Hartman was in 572. This headline-making event produced a new level of respect for the prop-driven Spad.

little above my altitude, flew toward me. Ed called for us to pickle our drop tanks so that we would have more maneuverability. In retrospect this was one of the most important decisions ever made—for me, anyway. I pressed the button on the control stick and the two 300-gallon tanks on either wing fell away. This sudden loss of weight and drag caused my Spad to actually leap upward, like a quickly rising elevator. At precisely that moment, bullets from the MiG zipped beneath me, their path through the sky signaled by tracer rounds, right where I was the instant before releasing the tanks. Clint later told me that when he saw the tanks and the gunfire he thought I'd been hit.''

Hartman and Johnson were at 500 feet now when a rather astonishing thing happened. The MiG that had just fired whizzed by the two Skyraiders, then banked sharply toward the north. No one is sure why. Perhaps he was running low on fuel. Johnson and Hartman were on the northern side of the formation, Greathouse and Lynne to the south near a karst ridge.

"They were being chased by the second MiG," said Hartman. "Ed and Jim were jinking rapidly. All of us were bucketing along at about 225 knots. The next few seconds was like being in a mixmaster. There was a swirling fight involving four or five full-circle turns with us trying to either stay out of the MiG's sights or get a shot at him. The MiG pulled up after about the fifth circle. He then rolled sharply to the left in order to get into position for a head-on pass at Greathouse and Lynne. As he sped toward them, Clint and I had a head-on shot at the MiG. We both fired our 20-millimeter cannons." (A post-flight check revealed that Hartman fired an estimated ninety rounds; Johnson, fifty.)

"I saw the canopy of the MiG shatter as the shells struck it and the fuselage, but the plane kept coming toward us, trailing a thin plume of flame and smoke," said Hartman. "The pilot was probably incapacitated because the MiG-17 actually flew between Clint and me, pretty much straight and level."

Then, as the Skyraider pilots looked on in a state of wonderment coupled with satisfaction, the wounded jet fell off on its wing and slammed into the karst ridge, erupting into a huge red and black fireball. The other MiG was last seen in the distance.

"That was it," said Hartman. "The whole affair lasted about three minutes. We joined up, excited as hell naturally, and headed back to the ship. It was dark when we landed."

Hartman believed that when the MiG made his tight turn to get a nose shot at Ed and Jim, he either lost sight of or forgot about Clint and himself. Of course, they would never know for sure.

For their actions, Johnson and Hartman, who marked his twenty-fifth birthday two days after the fight, were awarded Silver Stars; Greathouse and Lynne received Distinguished Flying Crosses. Ed Greathouse continued his naval career, becoming a captain before retiring. Clint Johnson left the service to become an airline pilot. Charlie Hartman, at this writing, is a commander still on active duty. Tragically, Jim Lynne, a highly respected aviator and solid citizen in every respect, lost his life in an airplane crash in Indonesia in the late 1970s. He had left the Navy after his Vietnam tour and was killed in a small aircraft while performing his duties as a flying missionary.

Lieutenant (Junior Grade) Nick Daramus had flown his last hop in VA-122, the West Coast's A-1 replacement training squadron. It was a Friday in June 1965, at the Naval Air Station in Fallon,

Skyraider

Nevada, where aircrews honed weapons delivery skills at target complexes located on the surrounding desert-like terrain. He was told he would have to leave in two days to join VA-25, "The Fist of the Fleet" squadron aboard the USS *Midway*, to replace a pilot and close friend, Lieutenant (Junior Grade) Carl Doughtie, who had been killed. The *Midway* was on Yankee Station when the young officer, toting flight gear, uniforms, and personal belongings, was delivered by COD aircraft.

His first flight, a rescue combat patrol, proved uneventful. Shortly thereafter the *Midway* retired to Yokosuka, Japan, for a scheduled respite from the action. A week or so later the ship was back in the Gulf of Tonkin, and Daramus got his first real test of combat. He was assigned as wingman for the C.O., Korean veteran and former prisoner of war Commander Harry Ettinger. Lieutenant Dennis Laack and Lieutenant (Junior Grade) Charlie Hartman, who had crossed swords victoriously with a MiG-17 a short time before, were in the flight. It turned out to be a six-hour-plus reconnaissance mission, during which each of the flyers destroyed a bridge.

"I had never dropped live ordnance from the center station of the Spad," said Daramus, "and was therefore unprepared for the severe jolt when the ejector foot fired and kicked away the 2,000-pound bomb I was aiming at a bridge. Smoke from the ejector cartridge filtered into the cockpit and though not abnormal, scared the hell out of me. Surely I'd been hit. I wanted to key the mike and tell the world of my problems. Thankfully, words wouldn't come. I was speechless. And believe it or not, the bomb hit the bridge."

Next day, 24 July 1965, Lieutenant "Abe" Abrahamson and Daramus launched on a routine rescap that became everything but routine. Not long after they were in the sky, Crown Alpha, an Air Force plane responsible for controlling rescue operations, wanted the two to provide cover and assistance for an F-105 pilot who had been hit and ejected in Laos while on a recce mission near Route One, a major enemy thoroughfare. Thunderstorms and multiple cloud layers reached up to 12,000 feet in the area. Abrahamson led the section through and got down under the clouds, which created a lid about 700 to 800 feet above the ground.

"We found ourselves in a relatively level, thickly forrested expanse," said Daramus. "But there were mountains and hills around us. We located the survivor although it took quite awhile even though he helped by transmitting to us on his survival radio. There's nothing quite so small and undetectable as a human being in the jungle. Abe and I had difficulty keeping each other in sight because of extremely poor visibility and the need to keep a wary eye on the terrain. It wouldn't do to smash into one of those hills."

Continued Daramus, "Fortunately, while the undergrowth was thick, it was not very high. It was characterized by lush, tall grass and large-leaved banana plants. We finally spotted the pilot, hiding under one of the banana plants. Once that was accomplished, we headed west to meet the inbound helo, a small Kaman type flown by the Air Force, I think it was. The actual pick-up was routine except for some intermittent ground fire which we were able to suppress with our 2.75-inch rockets and the cannons.

"Abe and I were about to escort the chopper out of the danger zone when Crown Alpha notified us that an A-6 Intruder, new to Yankee Station operations, flying from USS *Independence*, had just been bagged. Our helo pilot radioed his thanks and said, 'We can find our way home OK; don't worry about us.' So we departed for the Intruder crew, a pilot and his bombardier navigator (BN), down in an area which my charts verified was noted for heavy concentrations of triple-A and small-arms fire. It was a place to be avoided when possible. Today it wouldn't be possible.

"We picked our way through clouds and hills and were subject to some ground fire. The survivors had landed in a relatively large clearing, covered with square-shaped rice paddies, perhaps two miles across. The pilot was believed to be in a clump of small trees and plants near the center of the clearing. The BN was hiding amongst large trees along the edge of it. We established radio communications with them and determined that they were separated by about a quarter to a half mile, in relatively good physical condition except that the BN had a leg injury and was barely able to move. Aggravating the situation and increasing their already high level of anxiety was the sight of enemy ground forces heading in their direction.

"Things got a bit confusing," recalled Daramus. "We were trying to pinpoint the survivors' locations by radio. Had they used signal flares, they would have been like bright arrows pointing at their precise positions. They called out movements of the troops. Abe meanwhile was trying to transmit their location to Crown Alpha so that a helo could be summoned. We didn't know it right away, but two Marine Corps whirlybirds, based somewhere in South Vietnam, were on the way. At the same time Abe and I made coordinated rocket and strafing runs, covering each other from ground fire, and trying to hold the oncoming forces at bay. Finally, Abe determined that there was simply too much chatter on the air waves. 'You'll have to stay off the radio for a while,' he cautioned the survivors, 'or we won't be able to get you out.'"

Continued Daramus, "For about an hour we swooped and circled, effecting a stand-off with the enemy. We'd see people heading for the clearing from a nearby village. As they approached, Abe and I would roll in and strafe them. Rolling in was a job in itself because of the low overcast. It was most difficult to get a steep-enough dive angle for accuracy. We'd have to pop up into the clouds in our turns then poke down through, which didn't leave much time to track, aim, and fire a burst or two before pulling up.

"The Intruder crew were instrumental in their own rescue once we got the radio talk reduced. They would report 'On Top' when Abe and I flew directly over them, thus enhancing our ability to know exactly where they were. But, because they remained hidden in the foliage, we never did see them until they finally fired tracers from their .38-caliber pistols a little later."

Said Daramus, "Crown Alpha directed one of the helicopters into the clearing once he was convinced we had pinpointed the men on the ground. We had been on the scene for two hours when the choppers arrived. Abe and I were running low on ammo and were making nonfiring passes to keep enemy heads down and discourage them from moving toward the Americans. The second helo was also directed in. Abe took charge of one; I escorted the second. He was to go after the pilot. My responsibility was the BN. We told the guys on the ground to expose themselves at the last instant as the helos came in.

"I must admit that the action now resembled that of a cage of excited monkeys. We had the two survivors, two helicopters, and two Spad pilots—all talking on the same frequency, trying to achieve two separate pick-ups, within the same area, at the same time. We kept the helos over the heavily forested hills, reducing their exposure to a minimum, until they made a final dash in. The survivors left their sanctuaries at the right time even though they were reluctant to enter the clearing knowing the bad guys were nearby. The pilot got to his helo in short order and clambered aboard. The BN took longer because of his injury, but he, too, made it. We hustled out of there as fast as we could but found it impossible to stay with the choppers because of the terrain and the poor weather. The helo pilots assured us they could find their way home and motored off, unescorted, with two happy warriors on board. Abe and I joined up for the journey home. We logged 7.8 hours in the saddle that day. What a great airplane to do it in. With the Skyraider, it was a piece of cake!"

Because there was a policy to reduce the number of high-level awards pilots were receiving during this time, the two Spad Drivers received Air Medals for actions that certainly deserved consideration for Distinguished Flying Crosses. But to these two pros, satisfaction in saving three lives made the effort worthwhile. Daramus, a Naval Academy graduate, became an A-7 Corsair pilot and a commander after his Skyraider days. Abrahamson went on to duty as a flight instructor. He was killed while on a night training mission some time later.

There hardly was such a thing as an average or typical rescap evolution in Vietnam. Each had a character all its own. Three days after the adventure of Daramus and Abrahamson, Ed Greathouse and Jim Lynne found themselves on a rescue hop that, but for its inherently solemn nature, had comic aspects. The Air Force had flown a first-of-its-kind strike specifically aimed at a surface-to-air missile site, with unhappy results. Several F-105s were shot down either during the strike or en route to their home base in Thailand.

Remembered Greathouse, "Jim and I arrived for rescap duty around 1300, just as the last fighter was leaving the scene. There was only one 'evader' on the ground positioned about 30 miles west of Hanoi. Visibility was so good I could easily see the city and its airport from the area. There were several triple-A batteries in the immediate vicinity, but the pilot was on a good-sized ridge. We communicated with him, pinpointed his location, and told him to stay put, that we would leave the area so as to not give away his location to the enemy and return. We retired about 60 miles to the south, close to the Laotian border, to await a helicopter. Every hour or so we would return and talk with the downed pilot for a few minutes. Finally, about four P.M. we were advised that a helicopter was on the way but would be slow in coming because it had to refuel several times en route. It would arrive about dusk."

Once again the ability of the Skyraider to loiter, to stay with the action, to perform under the most arduous circumstances, was highlighted.

Continued Greathouse, "The Jolly Green chopper arrived at the North Vietnamese border unescorted and ready to go to work despite the fact that the pilot had no maps or knowledge of the area. Using our direction-finding gear we 'talked him' to our position near the Black River, spotted him, and escorted the helo to the ridge, arriving as darkness was setting in."

A flight of F-105s arrived at the same time. So did several enemy trucks and a number of ground troops. They gathered in the flat lands surrounding the high area that was the survivor's temporary sanctuary. The Jolly Green paid out 200 feet of the rescue cable, at the end of which was a hoisting device, down through the jungle canopy. This was tough work and demanded unswerving concentration in the face of the oncoming enemy, who were now proceeding toward the object of the helo's effort. The downed pilot got into the sling, and the aircrewmen quickly began reeling in the cable with its precious cargo.

To the anger and frustration of all naval and Air Force personnel, however, the cable became fouled. It wouldn't retract more than 50 feet. The survivor thus dangled precariously 150 feet below the Jolly Green. Greathouse had one descriptive word for the next 15 minutes: "Wild!" Night was falling. F-105s, the two Spads, and the chopper, not to mention a worried F-105 pilot no longer in the friendly confines of his cockpit, were deep in North Vietnamese territory, and enemy troops were closing in.

The helicopter pilot spotted what appeared to be an abandoned army camp nearby with barracks-type buildings and a parade ground. With the survivor hanging on for dear life, the pilot tried to land on the parade ground, but a flag pole, of all things, was so located as to preclude a safe touch down. The survivor got off the cable, and the helicopter motored to a rice paddy about 100 yards away. He tried to set his machine down there.

"The pilot sprinted toward the Jolly Green," said Greathouse. "But because of the mud and water the helo couldn't sit down. He moved away another 50 yards or so looking for a better spot." The pilot, more determined than ever to get aboard his chariot to safety, hot-footed it after the chopper in a race that would have challenged the most ardently trained Olympic runner.

"That pilot was really stepping high and splashing through there," marveled Greathouse. "The trucks were a mere quarter mile away rumbling toward the paddy. Jim and I and the F-105s kept them at bay with strafing runs."

Happily, the survivor made it to his chariot, scrambled aboard, and was lifted away. On the ground it was just about dark. Greathouse and Lynne escorted the helo to the Laotian border where, despite nightfall, the Jolly Green pilot told the Canastas he could make it on his own the rest of the way. The drained Spad Drivers then took up a heading for the sea and their carrier. They checked in with the *Midway* and were advised that since they had been in the air so long, they were to proceed to Danang, land there, and return to the ship next day.

Lieutenant (Junior Grade) Tom Patton of VA-176 stands on the wing of his Skyraider after bagging a MiG 17. Below his arm on fuselage is graphic of the Soviet fighter with an "X" drawn through it.

"This turned out to be the hairiest part of the mission," recalled Greathouse. "It was drizzling at Danang when we got there at about 2200, and the runway was wet. We had to make a steep approach. I had made only one field landing in the previous three and a half months and pulled the standard 'Spad-Pilot-Going-Ashore-Trick': I forgot to lock the tail wheel. [On carrier landings the tail wheel is unlocked. For field landings the reverse is true to enhance the landing roll-out. Greathouse's error was not unexpected under the circumstances. Ask any A-1 pilot.] I landed long and hot and almost lost my bird before coming to a stop a few feet before the end of the runway. Anyway, Jim and I made it safely. We had been airborne for 9.3 hours."

After Skyraider time in the war zone, incidentally, Ed Greathouse returned twice to Vietnam in the ensuing years as an A-7 Corsair pilot. On his last Yankee Stadium tour he was a Fist of the Fleet again in VA-25, a squadron that he eventually commanded. VA-25 had transitioned to A-7s after surrendering its A-1s in 1968.

"I have a feeling this flight is going to be different," Lieutenant Tom Patton said to himself. The twenty-six-year-old Skyraider pilot from Attack Squadron 176 aboard the USS *Intrepid* on Yankee Station was briefing with three wingmen for a special rescap mission.

It was 6 October 1966, nearly a year and a half after VA-25 bagged its MiG. The air war in Vietnam had intensified significantly, especially in the Hanoi and Haiphong areas. Alpha strikes, major attacks made by thirty or more aircraft and support planes, were occurring on a regular basis. Diving en masse, the naval and Air Force flyers weaved their way through horrible concentrations of flak and surface-to-air missiles to strike at designated targets. The opposition was so intense and the targets were so heavily defended that losses were inevitable.

The *Intrepid* had four attack squadrons, two A-4 Skyhawk and two Spad outfits. There were no fighter or support units on board. "With so many A-1s, planners weren't always sure what to do with us," recalled Patton. "Mostly we were turned loose and told to be careful. In my own case most of the targets I hit during forty missions over the north [he also had thirty-seven missions over the south] were of my own choosing. We frequently roamed at will, exercising our own judgment, hitting bridges, trucks, barges, and the like. We actually blew up two ammo depots and were involved in one 'mini' Alpha Strike."

On this day Tom Patton and his flight were to orbit offshore with a helicopter on standby rescue duty for a three-carrier strike against a target near Hanoi. Three separate Alpha Strike groups, one right after the other, were going in. The odds on losing a plane were high. The rescap flights were increased beyond the norm; Patton's division of four Skyraiders supplemented a two-plane section assigned a different location.

Lieutenant Commander Leo Cook, the operations officer in VA-176, was the flight leader, with Lieutenant (Junior Grade) Jim "Pud" Wiley on his wing and Lieutenant Pete Russell and Patton in the second section. The weather was clear, the sea relatively calm, and the launch and rendezvous with the helicopter were uneventful. There were some clouds over the mountains inland but not enough to preclude the strikes from proceeding.

Hugging the coastline southeast of Hanoi, the Spads circled for an hour and a half. "Looking at the no-man's land between us and the target, I wondered whether anyone in his right mind would even try to take four A-1s in there," said Patton. "If someone did go down, we'd have to take a direct route to save time, and the direct route would carry us over some deadly flak sites, not to mention SAM emplacements."

Patton had gone deep into "Indian Country," as Hanoi and its environs were sometimes called, on other missions, but always before his flights had enjoyed the luxury of selecting entry and exit points. They were able to dart their Skyraiders between and around most missile and triple-A areas. Not so today.

The jets swooped in on their attack as the Spads and helo orbited. Towers of brown-black smoke rose from the target, signifying bomb explosions. Soon jets were winging toward the east, not unlike ricocheting bullets, as pilots flew briskly toward the sanctuary of the sea. After a time it seemed that all the planes had survived the attack. Maybe they wouldn't have to go in after all, thought Patton.

Then an emergency transmission reported that a naval F-4 Phantom had been downed by ground fire, and its two-man crew had ejected about twenty miles southwest of Hanoi. Patton looked at his chart and the proliferation of dark circles representing enemy flak and SAM sites between the flight and the search-and-rescue scene. The area's terrain was characterized by saw-toothed mountains.

"I felt *we* could get in but worried about the helo's chances," said Patton. "He'd be a sitting duck." But the decision was made to proceed. Fellow flyers were in travail, and if there was any way the Spads could help, they at least had to try.

"I didn't envy Cook having to make the go-ahead decision," said Patton. "It was a long shot. But I admired his guts."

Cook and Wiley immediately went feet-dry [passed over land from the sea] and headed for the SAR site. Patton and Russell then began inland, Russell weaving in front of the helo, responsible for

Skyraider

navigation, and Patton in the rear, ready to pounce on any sources of ground fire. The flight was conducted at about eight to nine thousand feet, an altitude they hoped was high enough to keep the entourage above the triple A's most effective range. SAMs, of course, remained a very real threat. The helo was calculated to have enough fuel for a round-trip journey plus ten minutes on-station, or loiter, time. The Spads had plenty of gas, endurance being one of the aircraft's most precious commodities.

No sooner had Patton, Russell, and the helicopter penetrated the coastline than a fierce barrage of flak filled the sky. The multiple explosions of lethal white and black clouds were as thick and frightening as any Patton had seen.

"When I saw that first curtain of triple A, I thought it would be impossible for the helo to get through," he said. "The pilot must have felt that way, too. Either that, or he became disoriented. He had swung around to the east, pointed toward the water." At Patton's urging, however, he altered his course.

"I rolled in on the gun sites," said Patton. "I made several firing passes, scattering 20-millimeter cannon shells wildly. I thought the runs would keep a few North Vietnamese heads down, but there was no noticeable effect on the volume of flak. I think the runs boosted the helo crew's morale though. Also, I was careful to use only two of the four cannons. I wanted plenty of 20 mike mike on hand for possible use later on."

Continued Patton, "All of a sudden the shooting stopped. It was as if we had passed through a waterfall into the clear. We had made it unscathed, except for the helo, which took some hits but none serious enough to cancel the mission."

Shortly thereafter Lieutenant Commander Cook transmitted the unsettling news that four MiG-17s had been sighted in their area. Instinctively, Pete Russell radioed a destroyer offshore that was monitoring the action. He asked for immediate air cover. To the dismay of the Spad drivers, not only had all of the F-4 Phantoms and F-8 Crusaders designated for CAP (combat air patrol, or "cover") duty run low on fuel, but they were unable to locate an aerial tanker and replenish. It was clear that the A-1s, which at normal rated power in level flight could sustain about 240 knots, were about to encounter enemy fighters that could travel at nearly twice that speed with relative ease.

"I've got three MiGs taking turns on me," reported Jim Wiley excitedly. Then, in almost total frustration he pleaded, "Please get some fighter cover in here!"

"At this point," recalled Patton, "Pete Russell uttered words that ought to go down in the annals of warfare as a lasting tribute to the Skyraider. The words stand right up there with that World War II battle report made by another warrior, 'Sighted Sub, Sank Same!' Somehow, despite the pressure and dismal prospects of the moment, when Pete heard Wiley's urgent call for help, he was inspired to respond: *'Right, Pud . . . we're on our way with two Spads and a helo!'*"

In the melee near the SAR scene—a mountainous area above which there were some thick clouds—the quartet of MiGs had forced Wiley and Cook to separate. A single enemy fighter engaged Cook, but he was able to keep it at a standoff. Wiley was in deep trouble because the other three MiGs were rolling in on him from a racetrack pattern. He kept himself intact by skimming along the treetops and bending his machine around as close to the ground as possible. When Pud raced by a sharp mountain peak, he broke to the left. One of the MiGs, in close pursuit, whipped by it to the right, then banked steeply to the left, popping directly in front of Wiley, who let loose a burst of gunfire.

The 20 mike mike ripped off the tip of the MiG's wing, and a vapor trail streamed from it. Wiley was thus credited with a probable kill although no one saw the MiG actually crash.

"Pete and I arrived right after that with the helo," said Patton. "We were strung out, spotted two of the remaining MiGs, and maneuvered for a head-on pass." With all four cannons armed, Russell pressed his trigger, aiming at the belly of the lead MiG. So close did the aircraft pass that Russell's Spad shook momentarily from the fighter's wake. Although that MiG wasn't seen again, Russell was also credited with a possible kill.

It was now Patton's turn. He was still at 9,000 feet. Altitude was energy to him, and he knew he'd need all he could muster. He recounted: "I shoved the throttle forward to full power, then pushed over. A MiG, darting along above the trees, was heading in my direction but didn't see me. I counted three or four seconds until I figured he was in range, then rolled my Spad into a split-S. I dove straight down gathering speed to 350 and more knots and completed the split at the MiG's four o'clock position, pulling Gs to recover from the dive."

Patton's angle was a bit steep, but he fired a few rounds anyway.

The MiG pilot then spotted Patton's Skyraider and hauled his machine hard up toward it.

"Apparently, he judged that I would overshoot him," said Patton, "and executed a reverse turn. This was a fatal mistake on his part. He was climbing, dissipating speed, while I still had plenty. Maybe his reversal would have worked against another MiG-17, but in this case it was premature on his part because I ended up right behind him at his six o'clock. I'd been tight as a clenched fist till this point. But now I actually felt myself relax, knowing the advantage I had.

"I waited patiently until the MiG filled my gunsight reticle. This was, of course, the most exciting moment in my life. I'll never forget it. The most obvious first impression I had when up close to the enemy fighter was the 'coke bottle' shape of the fuselage. The only marking I remember was the red star midway on the fuselage. Both the MiG and I were climbing, me in close trail on him. I fired the cannons. My wings trembled, and the 20 mike mike sounded a reassuring, deep staccato as they streamed right into the tailpipe of the MiG. I was so close I could see metal fragments flying from the tail, which was literally disintegrating. I estimate that I commenced firing at about 500 feet and closed to approximately 100 feet, which is close! Both the MiG and I were pointed up at a 75-degree angle when all four of my guns quit. Two of the cannons were empty, I later learned; the other pair apparently jammed. The MiG still hadn't exploded so I actuated the rocket trigger and fired three Zunis, one right after the other." The five-inch rockets, designed for air-to-ground attack but highly regarded for their straight and true trajectory, burst from their pods mounted beneath the wings. They zoomed by the MiG, narrowly missing it.

Said Patton, "The MiG then flipped over and plummeted toward a mass of clouds below. I bent my aircraft around and followed him. Just before the MiG disappeared into the white mass, I fired the last rocket, which must have missed also. Enveloped by the clouds I switched my visual scan to the gages in order to right myself. I wasn't anxious to smash into one of the surrounding mountains. I popped clear at 500 feet and was bottoming out from the dive when off to my left I saw the pilot eject from the MiG."

Meanwhile, the helo was close by above the clouds and witnessed virtually all of the action but for the ejection and crash of the MiG, whereas Leo Cook and the others were about three miles away and saw none of the encounter but passed over the crash site shortly afterward. Patton received official credit for the kill. The combination of the helicopter crew's report and Cook's verification of the crash site left no doubt that Patton had joined the coveted honor roll of MiG-killers. The flyers learned later that a flight of four MiGs had launched against the Americans, but only three returned to land, one heavily damaged in the wing.

Patton with Lieutenant Pete Russell and VA-176 A-1 sporting distinctive Bumble Bee markings.

Patton believed it was his guns rather than the rockets that knocked the MiG from the sky. He commented, "I think the 20 mike mike disabled his engine. Maybe the MiG pilot made that last plunge through the clouds to reach a lower altitude for bailout. Perhaps he felt that punching out earlier would have made him a helpless target floating down in his chute."

Cook ordered Patton and Russell to escort the helo home while he and Pud Wiley again took up the search for the downed Phantom crew, an effort that eventually proved fruitless. The crew was never found.

It was a pleasant surprise for the Spad drivers, and the helo, to discover that their exit route was covered by dense clouds. Said Patton, "We penetrated them on a direct route to the sea and passed over the previously inhospitable area. The North Vietnamese may have expended their supply of artillery rounds and missiles earlier against the Alpha Strike groups."

There was a little more excitement left for the flight. "The poor helo was so low on fuel that it couldn't hold altitude," said Patton. "So we began a gradual descent through the soup, hoping intensely that we'd be over water rather than land when we broke out."

Skyraider

Happily, the group emerged from clouds a mile offshore and saw a U.S. naval destroyer, which had been alerted about the low fuel state of the whirlybird, closing toward the beach. The helo swooped down anxiously to the ship, set up a hover over the stern, and plugged into the aerial refueling apparatus. As the aircraft began gulping gas, the pilot saw his fuel indicator needle on the zero mark. They had made it with literally no fuel to spare.

"I had achieved my fondest dream, bagging a MiG," said Patton. I can tell you we were four very pumped up naval aviators as we formed a sharp-looking echelon, winged by the *Intrepid*, and hit the break for landing. We knew there would be a lot of attention focused on us because accounts of the engagement, although sketchy, had been passed to the ship."

In retrospect Patton said, "We firmly believed that as Spad drivers we could hack anything the jets could, only better. I know there have been many other examples of Skyraider achievements through the years. But I think our flight of October 6, 1966 demonstrated graphically just how great the Spad and the men who flew it could be."

For their performance, Lieutenant Tom Patton was honored with the Silver Star, while Wiley, Russell, and Cook received Distinguished Flying Crosses. Pete Russell, incidentally, completed the *Intrepid* cruise and returned to the United States for a time, only to volunteer for more combat duty in Vietnam flying OV-10 light attack aircraft. It was in this capacity that he was shot down and killed, fighting for his country, in South Vietnam.

In this photo celebrating fifty years of naval aviation are, top to bottom, the carriers *Intrepid*, *Saratoga*, and *Independence*. Despite desire in some quarters for "all-jet" air groups, the Skyraider lingered on, and, as shown here, each of these ships had an A-1 outfit on board. At the zenith of its career, forty-four squadrons in the Navy and Marine Corps were flying Skyraiders.

In this sequence a VA-176 A-1's wheels malfunctioned and couldn't be extended; so the pilot made a successful barrier engagement aboard the USS *Intrepid*, in 1966.

1

2

Torque, if not handled properly, could cause disastrous problems, especially in the near-stall, approach attitude.

5

3

4

6

This *Saratoga*-based AD-5Q was filmed in early 1960s. Of the 3,180 Skyraiders built, 670 were the AD-5 (later A-1E) type.

Underside view of Skyraider with five-inch HVARs on wing racks.

Marine Corps AD-5s sweep low over troops in practice exercises at Onslow Beach, N.C., in late 1950s.

Landing signal officer "cuts" AD-5 during field carrier landing practice at Brown Field, San Diego, in 1954.

EA-1 of VAW-33 launches from the *Independence*'s number two catapult during Mediterranean exercises, 1964.

Able Dog could even lay a smoke screen, as shown in this picture of Aviation Training Group 182 Skyraiders off the Virginia Beach, Va. coast in 1957.

The USS *Essex* transits Suez Canal en route to Seventh Fleet in the Pacific after supporting landings of U.S. Marine Corps troops in Lebanon with the Sixth Fleet in the late 1950s. ADs share deck space with jets and AJ Savage heavy attack bombers on left.

Then and now: AD-4, number 168, bearing Navy Atlanta markings is shown aloft in the 1950s. Captain Harry Ettinger, long-time Skyraider pilot, provided the picture. On the ground in recent years is 168, having been faithfully refurbished by Mr. Dave Forrest.

One of Knoizen's VA-165 Spads loaded with depth charges launches from the USS *Intrepid* on Yankee Station, May 1966. Conical tips on 20-millimeter cannons were flash hiders.

Jim Fausz has a warm spot for old number 178, which is still around. (Fausz)

VA-165's Jim Parrie examines damaged wing.

Skyraiders carried an almost unlimited variety of weapons over the years. This Naval Air Test Center, Patuxent River, Md. bird has Mark 36 and Mark 50 mines on the wings and main pylons.

VA-145 A-1 from the USS *Constellation* makes a deck run in 1963.

7

Down the Tube

The journey of a lifetime took about fifteen seconds as Myers successfully made his way across the stretch of hell on earth. Bullets zinged everywhere. The staccato of automatic weapons crackled all over the field. The deep buzz of the swooping Skyraiders accentuated the raw noise of combat.

Scene at A Shau Special
Forces Camp, South Vietnam,
March 1966

The Skyraider came late to the U.S. Air Force in comparison to the Navy's association with the attack bomber, but it wrote some exceptionally illuminating and inspiring chapters in the history of aerial combat during its tour with the men in blue. Naval Lieutenant Ken Moranville, with an assist from Hank Suerstedt and Admiral Don Felt, helped introduce the A-1 to Southeast Asia in 1960. Subsequently, the U.S. Air Force's Special Air Warfare Center at Hurlburt Field, Florida evaluated counter-insurgency (COIN) type aircraft. After exhaustive tests, officials concluded that the A-1E Skyraider was very well suited for the fighting, which was still going on and was expected to continue in the jungles, on the plains, and across the mountains of Vietnam.

A large number of the multi-place Spads were transferred from the Navy to the Air Force, with certain modifications. Dual control systems were incorporated in the birds so that they could be flown from either seat up front. (Originally in Vietnam the U.S. Air Force flyers were to function in an advisory capacity, with Vietnamese co-pilots responsible for identifying targets and deciding whether or not to attack them.) In anticipation of the need for maximum

Bernie Fisher and Wayne Myers are a pair of happy professionals after the incredible mission. (USAF)

communications capability in close air support and rescue operations, UHF, VHF, and FM radios were installed. (Later, the "Yankee" extraction seat was incorporated on Air Force and Navy A-1s. Somewhat uncomfortable compared to what Spad pilots were used to, it was designed for low-level emergency escape. Upon actuation, a rocket behind the seat would move to the erect position and fire the pilot out of the cockpit by the risers of his parachute. The canopy blossomed automatically. Even if upside down, the system was designed to "extract" the flyer and immediately place him upright in relation to the ground prior to his descent.) Meanwhile "straight" A-1Hs were transported across the Pacific to augment the South Vietnamese Air Force.

The A-1Es joined the fray in 1964. The U.S. Air Force's 602nd Fighter Squadron (Commando) and First Air Commando Squadron trained Vietnamese pilots at Bien Hoa in the manner of Ken Moranville. In August 1964 the Navy officially entered the fighting with retaliatory raids against PT boat bases in the Gulf of Tonkin (see Chapter 5), and in 1965 the roles of the commando squadrons changed as regular U.S. ground combat units began to proliferate in South Vietnam. Restrictions were lifted so that U.S. Air Force pilots, primarily tasked with training the Vietnamese, could now fly on combat missions without a Vietnamese pilot on board.

For the most part, the earlier Spad drivers were highly experienced Air Force fighter pilots. Although they were used to making 450-knot sweeps with jets, they adapted well to the stable Spad with its 300-knot speed in diving runs. Although unofficial, new standards for weapons accuracy were implemented, so accurate was the Spad if flown properly. On strafing runs, pilots strived to score at least 90 percent coverage of the target with the twenty-millimeter cannons. If a bomb struck beyond the twenty-foot circle, the pilot was chided for "needing a little more work."

Forward air controllers (FACs), some of whom flew A-1s, would typically call in available jets to bombard a target. The jets would make a run or two and within minutes be on their way home. A-1Es, on the other hand, were then summoned to work over the target, sometimes for hours on end. They used bombs, rockets, napalm, cluster bomblet units, and the cannons.

From the beginning these shore-based Skyraiders were proving as valuable as those that launched from the flattops. They mastered close-air-support assignments, striking targets within mere yards of friendly forces. In rescue operations, the Air Force Skyraiders were nothing short of magnificent. Accounts of the legendary

"Sandy" rescue missions could fill a book of encyclopedic proportions. Flying both A-1Es and, later in the war, the single-seat A-1s, the Sandys time and again saved lives. Their achievements were enthralling.

By August 1965, A-1Es were escorting helicopters on rescue flights, using techniques similar to the Navy's. Typical ordnance loads included bombs, rockets, white phosphorous charges for marking targets or survivor locations, and guns. Often the Spads carried a centerline fuel tank, a second fuel tank on one wing stub, and a 7.62 mini-gun on the other main pylon. A pair of Skyraiders would search for and locate the downed flyer(s) while a second section escorted the helicopter to the scene, protecting it from ground fire. Of course, few, if any, rescue evolutions adhered to a simple in-and-out sequence of events. Improvisation was the key, along with sound basic air work and an abundant supply of courage.

As the war wore on, heavily armed Skyraiders were taking off from runways at Pleiku, Da Nang, Udorn and Nakhom Phanom in Thailand, and many other places. They were never far from the fighting, and on a day-in, day-out basis were as familiar to the combatants as an infantryman's rifle. South Vietnamese Air Force pilots, to be sure, also piloted the Skyraider with skill and daring

U.S. Air Force Operations Squadron A-1 carries bombs, a centerline fuel tank, signal flares—handy during rescue and spotter missions—on outer wing racks. PHCS Bob Lawson, now editor of *The Hook*, the voice of the Tailhook Association, took this picture at Da Nang, South Vietnam, November 1968.

throughout the war, some of them accumulating incredible amounts of flight time—2,000, 3,000, and even 4,000 *combat* hours.

When the final tallies were in after the hostilities ended, it was calculated that U.S. Air Force Skyraiders participated in the rescue of more than 1,000 downed airmen.

Early in 1966, just three days after Tom Patton got his MiG up north, a different sort of action took place in South Vietnam, one destined to make headlines. North Vietnamese regulars had been infiltrating across the Laotian border only three miles from the U.S. Special Forces camp in the A Shau Valley. The Reds didn't appreciate the existence of the observation and harassing post; thus, on the ninth of March, they laid siege to it, with, reportedly, about 2,000 Vietcong troops.

The camp was located at the eastern edge of the valley, 70 miles west–northwest of Da Nang. Triangular in shape, it featured a 2,500-foot landing strip made of pierced steel planking. The valley itself was six miles long and a mile across.

Weather favored the Communists. Clouds extended from a low 200 feet all the way to 8,000, cloaking some of the mountain peaks and precluding easy access to the fort by support aircraft. Nevertheless, a few A-1s were sent to A Shau and began looking for a break in the clouds.

U.S. Air Force Major Bernard "Bernie" Fisher, a veteran jet pilot who had volunteered for combat duty and was assigned to the First Air Commando Squadron at Pleiku, was flying one of his unit's prop-driven A-1Es. A Mormon, father of five, and skilled aviator (being one of the few flyers ever to "dead-stick" a stub wing F-104 jet to a landing after an engine failure—indeed, he did it twice), he was on a routine mission when he was diverted to A Shau to join the other A-1s. On arrival over the camp he somehow found a light spot in the clouds and descended through the murky mass. Maneuvering his Skyraider with absolute precision, he made strafing passes against the Vietcong. His co-pilot in the right seat, Captain Robert Blood, although new to Vietnam, was highly impressed by the way Fisher was able to steeply bank the Skyraider and make his attacks within the confined space. The Red troops, however, were engaged in a furious, relentless assault, and the beleaguered holdouts in the camp were in a bad way.

Fisher went back up through the clouds several times to lead the waiting A-1s down. Their suppression fire was effective, but clearly a massive effort was needed—the fall of the camp was almost inevitable. At day's end the struggle was continuing.

Air Force pilot in A-1E Skyraider during practice mission gives a thumbs-up from the cockpit. Note cannons from accompanying aircraft poking out from lower right corner of picture. (USAF)

Next morning Bernie Fisher manned a different A-1E, number 649. He noted with pleasure the brand-new tires, the fourteen 100-pound bombs on the pylons, and the exceptionally clean cockpit. The crew chief, a Sergeant Suso, had even Simonized the control console. Filling out a form, Fisher noted that "This is the cleanest airplane I have ever seen." Skyraiders, of course, tended to be smudged with grease and oil unlike their jet-propelled brothers, so an immaculate-looking A-1 would tend to elicit praise.

With Captain Francisco "Paco" Vazquez in another Skyraider on his wing (he didn't have a co-pilot this time), Fisher launched. They were soon diverted from their assigned mission and sent to A Shau, where clouds still filled much of the sky above the fort. Four other Skyraiders were loitering above the overcast trying to get down through it. Once again Fisher found an opening. Leaving two of the

Spads to orbit in reserve, he led down three of the attack bombers. Flying in one of them was Major Dafford Wayne "Jump" Myers, call sign "Surf 41." Skipper of a detachment from the 602nd Fighter Squadron based at Qui Nhon, he was an acquaintance of Fisher's from earlier days when they had flown jets with the Air Defense Command.

Fisher brought the flight through the valley, a perilous passage that flyers had come to call the "tube." By now the enemy had established twenty or so AAA emplacements along the ridge lines on either side of the tube, and with almost shooting-gallery ease, fired away at the A-1Es as they funneled through. Evasive movements were severely restricted by the walls of the valley and the low-hanging clouds. Captain Hubert King, one of the three wingmen, took a hit in the canopy that shattered the glass so badly he had to leave, while Fisher, Myers, and Vazquez remained at the scene.

A Special Forces radio operator in the camp asked the Skyraiders to attack the fort's southern edge, which was being overrun. The Spads swung into action and began making their runs. As Myers was pulling up from his second pass, a stream of automatic weapons fire, possibly thirty-seven-millimeter, tore through his Wright R-3350.

He transmitted, "I've been hit, and hit hard." Later he recalled that "The engine started sputtering and cutting out, and then conked out for good." Fisher, in "Hobo 51," saw Myers's bird aflame from nose to tail. It was clear that Jump was too low to bail out and that he had no choice but to try to crash-land. As he descended, Myers observed, "I'll have to put her down on the strip."

Fisher issued brief directions to Myers, whose vision was curtailed by the smoke-filled cockpit. He was able to get the airplane on the ground but was "hot"—a little fast. Fisher advised him to raise his wheels. Jump did so and bellied in, but the centerline fuel tank exploded on impact. Surf 41 slid the length of a football field before smashing into an embankment.

The Skyraider was engulfed in flames. It took Myers a perilous minute or so, almost miraculously, to unhitch his seat harness, shed his encumbering survival gear, and, in flight suit only, roll back the canopy. He spotted an opening through the flame that looked like a "path through the Red Sea"—apparently it had been created by a blessed wind. He got onto the Skyraider's wing, ran to its edge, and leaped into a patch of weeds.

What Myers saw from his new, ground-level perspective was a grotesque still life of combat. Debris was everywhere. Even the weeds seemed to have been seared by the gunfire and the heat of exploding grenades. Shell casings, unused bombs, chunks of wood, splotches of oil, fuel drums punctured with bullet holes, rocket pods—all were strewn about. Jagged strips of runway planking jutted up dangerously from the turf.

Fisher immediately called for a rescue helicopter, even though at first he had to wonder if Myers was ever going to get out of the plane. Then he saw Jump scrambling away from the stricken machine, smoke pouring from his flight suit. He was alive!

The Skyraiders were hitting either side of the runway as well as the rise to the east, from which poured a hail of fire. Although Vazquez's plane was hit by bullets, he stayed on the scene. Control, the rescue unit, asked Fisher if he could poke up through the clouds to guide the helicopter when it arrived. Fisher learned that the chopper's ETA was still many minutes away.

"I couldn't go off looking for a chopper," said Fisher. "I told Control that I was going in to get the pilot." He then directed Captains Jon Lucas and Dennis Hague, in the A-1s that had been holding to the north, to come in and provide suppression fire with Vazquez. He was going to land and try to get Myers out. The three covering Skyraiders set up a tight pattern so that every fifteen or so seconds one of them was bearing down on the enemy, to keep their heads low while Fisher did his thing.

By now Myers was at some distance from his disintegrating plane. He recalled, "I was hiding against an embankment ten feet high just west of the runway. There was at least a company of enemy troops on top of the bank, but they couldn't see me. Also, I think that they thought I was dead."

Myers did indeed think his number might be up. A Shau was swarming with Vietcong—a helicopter couldn't possibly get through such a concentration of enemy guns. He said, "It never occurred to me that somebody would be crazy enough to put an A-1E down on that strip." Not only would a landing aircraft be the focus of all kinds of gunfire, but the torn planking, mortar holes, and other random obstacles could wreak havoc with the wheels, not to mention other parts of the aircraft.

Fisher released a final string of bombs west of the landing path. Moments before he had asked himself the inevitable, agonizing question: Could he rescue Jump Myers? His answer: He thought he could. A fellow American fighting man was in trouble, and there was absolutely no doubt that he, Major Bernard Fisher, must take whatever action he could to help.

Skyraider

He flew north, then turned back on a final approach to the south. As he eased back on the power, descending, a gust of wind set a billowing cloud of smoke across the runway, raising temporary hell with the visibility. That danger passed quickly, but Fisher realized he was too fast to land. He touched down briefly but jammed the throttle forward and took off again for another try.

"I bent it around real tight in a tear-drop turn and came in from the south holding it right at 95 knots," he said, 95 knots being a key speed for short-field landings. What Fisher achieved in the next few moments is the stuff of legend. No single landing of all the hundreds upon hundreds of thousands made in Skyraiders could surpass it for sheer drama.

As soon as the main mounts struck the ground, with the tail still up, he began tapping the brakes. He raised the flaps to get more weight on the wheels. He jockeyed the machine around mortar holes, not worrying about the rocket pods in his way, some of which hit the machine only to be booted away.

Said Fisher, "I saw the end of the runway coming up much too fast. That was the first time all day I was scared." He had but an instant to decide between hitting the brakes real hard, risking nosing up and grounding his prop into the turf, or running off the end of the runway. He elected the latter course. Fortunately, he ran into an accommodating patch of grass and soft dirt.

In a maneuver reminiscent of Ken Moranville's before a gathering of South Vietnamese VIPs six years earlier—but under far less auspicious circumstances—Fisher applied left brake and swung the Spad around. He then pushed on the power to taxi back up the runway. Jump Myers, a forlorn figure in the underbrush, waved unseen at him. Fisher brought the attack bomber to a stop at a point about seventy yards away from Myers and activated the parking brake. Rapidly, he began to unstrap so he could get out and retrieve Myers. Bullets were plunking into the Skyraider (ground crews later counted nineteen holes in the aircraft). One ripped into the plane a mere two feet from his head.

Meanwhile, Vazquez, Lucas, and Hague were roaring over the field. Even with ammo depleted, they made dry runs. (Lucas, in fact, took a hit, and his cockpit filled with smoke, but he refused to leave.) It would take a while for the enemy troops to realize the Skyraiders' guns were empty. Besides, the head-on spectre of a Spad, not to mention three of them, bearing down on a foe with its huge prop slicing through the sky, accompanied by the awesome sound of a 2,700-horsepower engine laboring mightily, is frightening enough

Artist's drawing of the fantastic rescue at A Shau in 1966 that earned Air Force Major Bernie Fisher the Medal of Honor. (USAF)

with or without fire spitting from the wing cannons. Heads tend to duck.

Myers was both amazed and puzzled about what was happening. He realized almost as in a surrealistic dream that Fisher was putting his tail on the line to save him despite overwhelming odds. Jump, who hadn't been a bad sprinter in his younger days, had to act. He emerged from the weeds and ran as fast as his forty-six-year-old legs could carry him, toward the Skyraider. The journey of a lifetime took about fifteen seconds as Myers successfully made his way across the stretch of hell on earth. Bullets zinged everywhere. The staccato of automatic weapons crackled all over the field. The deep buzz of the swooping Skyraiders accentuated the raw noise of combat.

Fisher was just about to leave the cockpit when he looked aft and was astonished to see Myers hauling himself up the trailing edge of the A-1E's wing. It was Jump's eyes that startled Fisher the most. They were red from the painful smoke—so red, in fact, that Fisher thought they "looked like neons."

Myers clambered across the wing. He reached the edge of the cockpit, pulled himself up, and dove in head first. Fisher grabbed hold and helped right him. Then, quickly, Fisher released the hand brake, arced the Skyraider around, and poured the coals to the R-3350.

The A-1E, number 649, did not let the men down. Fisher "danced" his way around the mortar holes, gathering speed. The tires somehow retained their tread despite the wicked torn planking. The plane lumbered down the runway and at the very end of the strip rose into the sky. The Vietcong must have been incredulous.

Said Fisher, "I held her right down on the bottom of the valley until we got out of the tube. Then I just took her right up through the hole in the clouds and leveled off."

Without a helmet, Myers could not talk to the man who had plucked him from the jaws of calamity. But he hugged Fisher momentarily and held up his hand, finger extended, signaling "Number One!" Caked with mud, Myers was a dismal sight. Nor did the smoke from his flight suit favorably enhance the smell inside the cockpit.

But this had to be one of the grand and enduring pictures of combat aviation: Bernie Fisher and Jump Myers, a pair of pros who had just pulled off a feat nothing short of astounding, primed to new heights of elation, were flying to safety, side by side, in a banged up, single-engine propeller-powered aircraft. As Fisher said, "We couldn't help turning to each other and laughing all the way home to Pleiku."

Lucas and the others made it back as well. His was a hydraulic fire, and by actuating a bypass valve, Lucas had managed to get the fire under control until reaching base. Special Forces advisors were given orders that afternoon to evacuate the camp, and in the next two days helicopters rescued survivors of the seige. Fisher and Myers touched down at Pleiku about one in the afternoon. Jump was in good physical shape but for the eyes, which a flight surgeon promptly treated.

Both Fisher and Myers emphatically credited the action of their wingmen, who suppressed the enemy during the critical moments of the rescue, with paving the way to freedom. All the participants were cited for their bravery. Contemplating some way he could at least partially thank Fisher, Myers initially wanted to give him a year's supply of whiskey. But that wouldn't do. Being a Mormon, Fisher didn't drink, not even coffee. On the other hand, he was a photography buff; so Myers bought him a camera.

Major Bernie Fisher became the first U.S. Air Force man to earn the Medal of Honor in Vietnam. It was presented to him in January

1967 by President Johnson at the White House. The hero of A Shau went back to flying jets after his Vietnam duty and eventually retired as a colonel to his home town of Kuna, Idaho.

Another of the approximately 1,000 downed flyers who were indebted, at least in part, to U.S. Air Force Spad drivers for their survival was an Air Force F-4 Phantom pilot. He made it to safety because of a Norfolk, Virginia native and West Point graduate named William A. Jones III.

On 1 September 1968, Lieutenant Colonel Jones was at the controls of his A-1H over North Vietnam leading a flight in search of the Phantom flyer. The scene was a mountainous area near Dong Hoi in the southern portion of North Vietnam. A FAC advised Jones that there was thirty-seven-millimeter and other automatic weapons fire active in the area. Hardly had this word come through when Jones's Spad was hit. Smoke entered the cockpit but cleared away, and he continued the search.

He sighted the pilot at about the same time he observed a multiple-barrel gun shooting at his A-1 from a position perilously close to the downed man. Apparently, the Red gunners had not yet seen the survivor. Jones made a pass, firing his cannons and some rockets. He maneuvered for a second run, and as he attacked was struck again. Automatic weapons fire ripped through his A-1H. Flames erupted in the cockpit, and a major section of his windshield was blown away. He actuated the ejection ("extraction") seat, but it must have been damaged because it failed to function. Jones was severely burned by the flames.

His wingmen repeatedly told him to bail out of his machine, but Jones began to climb to altitude intent on reporting the pilot's location and, equally important, the fact that the menacing enemy gun nearby had to be disabled if the rescue was to proceed. However, his transmissions couldn't be heard. They were blocked by the calls insisting that he vacate the aircraft.

By the time the cockpit fire burned itself out, all of Jones's transmitters were off the line. He could receive, but only on a single frequency. At altitude, determined to ride out the mission, he gave hand signals to his wingman indicating he would fly to home base about 100 miles away. Jones was convinced that this was the only way he could be sure to pass on the critical information about the F-4 pilot. He switched positions with his wingman and followed him in close formation through instrument weather conditions to the airfield. In fact, they had to make a ground-controlled approach through the clouds to a landing.

Skyraider

Badly injured, Jones had to be helped from the cockpit. But his first concern was the Phantom pilot. He detailed the pilot's location and emphasized the need to wipe out the gun position close to the man on the ground. As a direct result of Jones's information, the gun was destroyed later that day and the pilot saved.

Jones was returned to the United States for medical treatment, where he recovered from his injuries. A year later he was promoted to full colonel. In November 1969 he was on duty at Andrews Air Force Base outside Washington, D.C., when he was killed in the crash of his private plane. Just the day before he died, Jones had received his first copy of a book he had written and illustrated, *Maxims for Men-at-Arms*, a collection of quotations by eminent personalities about the military profession, gathered during his Air Force career.

In August of 1970, President Richard Nixon posthumously awarded Colonel Jones the Medal of Honor for his actions that day near Dong Hoi, North Vietnam.

8

Sea Stories and Farewell

> You know, I sort of feel like the Indian and the buffalo. I can see the sun going down.
>
> —Long-time Skyraider pilot,
> Lieutenant Commander Ralph Smith,
> in 1968, reflecting on the demise
> of the A-1

Every aircraft that ever left the ground has had its advocates as well as its detractors. If the former decisively outnumber the latter, the airplane becomes what Ed Heinemann calls "a winner." That the A-1 Skyraider was clearly and dramatically an overwhelming favorite, and thus a winner, is testimony to Heinemann's genius, the skilled contributions of his associates at Douglas Aircraft, the flyers who operated it, the troops who maintained it, and that wonderful, if unseen, cadre of aviation buffs, modelers, historians, and the like, around the world, who help sustain the legend. The following are a few footnotes sea stories and other tales, handed down through the years by folks who will always treasure these memories. Most are unquestionably true. A few aren't substantiated by proper documentation. But then, considering its lifetime and the countless individuals who knew the Able Dog, how many untold stories are there—countless vignettes that would further fuel the legend of the attack bomber that could do so much more than attack and bomb?

The question has been asked more than once: Can the Skyraider fly with its wings folded? The answer is a qualified yes. It can fly, but not with style.

VA-65 A-1s loaded with bombs await launch from the nuclear-powered USS *Enterprise* in late 1962. Skyraiders have taken off unintentionally from shore fields with wings folded like this and reached low altitudes before falling to the ground.

Skyraider

The scene: Naval Air Auxiliary Station Charlestown, Rhode Island, 1949. The pilot of an AD-2 had completed his engine checks and was cleared for takeoff on runway 22. He had left the flight line with his wings folded, intending to extend them on the way to the approach end of the duty strip. He jockeyed into position, adjusted his alignment with the compass heading of 22 degrees, and added power.

The airfield was quite busy at the time. In fact, not far away a landing signal officer working with another group of planes noticed the AD-2 with its wings up.

"Quick, call that pilot," he shouted to the radioman at his side. "Tell him to spread his wings."

In the control tower an alert sailor did likewise. The Skyraider began to roll forward.

Four times the controller in the tower called desperately as the Skyraider lumbered on, oblivious to its configuration. At the end of the fourth plea the man in the tower rang the crash phone.

The aircraft, meanwhile, gathered speed. It left the ground at the 2,800-foot point and gradually gained altitude. The LSO watched incredulously. The Skyraider was flying!

At this point the pilot was still unaware of any malfunction. "The takeoff roll seemed normal to me," he said later. "There was no sense of alarm." The Able Dog rose to about 250 feet and appeared to make a right turn. Then it fell off into a sharp left bank. The pilot vigorously applied right aileron and right rudder and somehow got the machine straight and level.

"I thought I had gone through some slipstream from another aircraft," he said. "There were other planes in the approach pattern performing field carrier landing practice [FCLP]." His reasoning held some logic. Suddenly, the aircraft banked again. This time it refused to return to level flight despite the pilot's frantic efforts. Startled now, he whipped his head back to his left and then to the right. With a sinking heart, he saw that his wings were folded.

This second steep bank caused a stall, and the Skyraider began to settle clumsily toward the ground. There are few sadder or more frightening sights than an airplane falling out of control toward the earth. Impact occurred at a forward speed of about 135 knots with full power on and wheels and flaps up. The AD hit the ground on its left wing stub, slid nearly the length of a football field before stopping, then burst into flames. The pilot managed to extricate himself from the wreckage and suffered only slight burns. No record exists of what disciplinary action, if any, the pilot received. But for a while at least his reputation as an airman suffered. As to the AD's reputation, officials were inclined to praise rather than malign it. After all, it did fly, even with the wings forming an inverted V over the cockpit.

This author must confess that but for the grace of a higher power, luck, or some mysterious inner instinct, I might have suffered a similar fate. It was a cloudless, sunny day in Naples, Italy, 1961. I had been sent to the beach from the carrier *Forrestal* to collect an AD and return it to the ship, but hadn't flown from a shore field in a long time. (On board the carrier, flight deck directors signaled pilots when to spread and fold their wings.) It was a quiet morning at the field, and no other aircraft were operating. I taxied to the runway, passing directly by and in clear view of the control tower, which was manned by a number of contented Italians who waved happily. To them nothing was awry with the Skyraider, whose wings were in that inverted V position.

I taxied onto the active runway after pre-takeoff checks were complete and all instruments indicated normal, then advanced the throttle to 30 inches of manifold pressure, checked the gages again, and released the brakes. The Skyraider lurched forward.

Perhaps it was a change in the light pattern on the instrument panel as the aircraft began to move. A sort of shadow was created by the angle of the upfolded wing and the way the sun shone upon it. Maybe it was a voice from the subconscious that said, "Something's wrong." More likely, luck saved me. Anyway, I retarded the throttle and hit the brakes. A nervous upward glance showed that, sure enough, those wings were folded.

Within seconds, without explaining matters to the Italians in the tower, I sheepishly spread the wings, closed the handle that retracted the red-colored locking rods called "beer cans," on either wing, and "re-executed" the takeoff—profusely thanking the man upstairs for getting me off what surely would have been a painful hook.

Incidentally, others have launched with their Skyraider wings folded and survived. According to Juan Santos, Jr., whose leatherneck father worked on ADs in Korea, a pilot launched from K-9 without spreading the wings but bailed out to safety before the plane crashed.

Richard M. Green, who later became an officer, was an aircrewman in VC-35. He recalled, "On 11 May 1951, in what may well be a world's record lift for a wingless aircraft, I rode as a radar operator [just he and the pilot were on board] in an AD-4N that climbed to

Skyraider

250 feet from the very short strip at Kangnung, Korea (K-18), with the wings neatly folded and hung with six 260-pound fragmentation bombs plus a full load of 20-millimeter ammunition." The aircraft sunk to the ground, crashed, and seemed to disintegrate, leaving only the fuselage intact. "But the pilot and I walked away from the resulting 'hard' landing," said Green, who credited the ruggedness of the Skyraider with his survival.

The spirit that prevailed among Skyraider operators has been manifested in diverse ways through the years. When eight ensigns from the *Valley Forge's* VF-194 were promoted to lieutenant (junior grade), they celebrated by staging an "all-ensign" air strike the day before they were to don the silver bars that replaced the gold ones on their collars. Each carried 4,000 pounds of bombs. They planned their missions, elected a flight leader, and went after railroad tracks and bridges in North Korea. Ensign Charles Brown led the attack. With him were Stan Broughton, Joe Molnar, Ken Wittman, Joe Akagi, Dean Hofferth, Robert Miller, and Frank Melton.

Then there's the case of the junior officers in VA-145 in 1953. Their outfit was deployed to El Centro near the California–Mexican border for training. The ensigns and lieutenants (junior grade) comprised half the squadron's complement of pilots. Their youth may or may not have accounted for their bravado. Perhaps they were genuinely confident. Anyway, all fourteen of them decided to become jump-qualified. They underwent the necessary period of instruction (such training was a specialty at El Centro), and went aloft on graduation day in the Navy Parachute Unit's R4D. In sequence they hurled themselves into the sunny skies.

All fourteen parachutes blossomed perfectly, and though a few bruises were sustained, it was an altogether memorable event. "Why did you do it?," the men were asked. The collective answer: "To find out how if felt." "How did it feel?" The response: "Well, it erased the fear of bailing out. One day, if there's a choice between going over the side or staying with the aircraft, it may save us from the hazards of ditching in rough terrain."

Highly experienced Skyraider pilot Captain R. R. Worchesek recalled the story of Ensign John Jacobs in VA-45 aboard the USS *Oriskany* in the Mediterranean in 1951: "Jacobs was catapulted on a daylight launch. Shortly after becoming airborne in his AD-2 he called MAYDAY!, saying that his engine was cutting out. He couldn't keep the plane airborne and was ready to ditch.

"As he raised the nose to a ditching attitude, his engine started again so he climbed to an altitude of several hundred feet and turned downwind to recover aboard the carrier as soon as possible. As he leveled off, his engine again quit and he lost altitude. He again prepared to ditch, but as he raised the nose to the ditching attitude, his engine started and off he went. The same series of events occurred several more times before Jacobs finally and very skillfully landed. Fuel was pouring out of the bottom of the aircraft."

Continued Worchesek, "Maintenance investigation revealed what had happened. On the cat shot part of the supporting mechanism of the 360-gallon rubber fuel bag in the fuselage gave way, causing the main fuel inlet hose to the engine to pull out of the bag. The main fuel outlet hose dropped to the aircraft bilge where fuel from the bag was pouring. Every time Ensign Jacobs raised the nose to land, the fuel sloshed in such a way that it covered the end of the inlet hose allowing the engine to start again. When he gained altitude and leveled off, the open end of the fuel inlet hose was uncovered, and the engine stopped."

Ken Knoizen could fly the Skyraider in his sleep. There are 4,000 A-1 hours inked in his log books along with 500 carrier landings—100 at night—and a lot of combat time. He flew every model of the A-1 and operated from more than a dozen carriers during a career that carried him to flag rank. Among many key posts, operational and staff, he was executive assistant to the chairman of the Joint Chiefs of Staff, Admiral Thomas H. Moorer; commander Naval Forces Caribbean; and chief of legislative affairs in Washington. Not bad for a Spad driver.

Having got in on the tail end of the Korean conflict, he recalled the time a bomb went where it wasn't supposed to, yet reaped abundant dividends. He was in VA-45, the "Blackbird" squadron, flying AD-4s off the USS *Lake Champlain*, the same outfit as Gus Kinnear (who once flew with his scarf tied to the control stick to keep aloft).

"Six of us had dropped 2,000 pounders on a target over the north and were returning to the ship," said Knoizen (pronounced Ka noy' zen). "Walt Clark was unable to release his even after four runs, however. He was worried, and rightly so, about getting aboard the ship with that excess load of TNT slung underneath him. We were level at 10,000 feet, and Walt kept jiggling his plane with rudder and ailerons, hoping the weapon would drop off. After a time it broke loose and sailed away. It hit a group of buildings. There followed the biggest explosion I'd ever seen. Walt had unintentionally blasted one of the enemy's major ammunition dumps. He got an Air Medal

Skyraider

for his achievement, but we never let him live down the way he earned it." (Perhaps incidents like this, coupled with the AD's capacity for delivering a broad assortment of weaponry, led to another nickname for the machine—the flying dump truck.)

The *Lake Champlain* stayed on after the hostilities ceased. In one exercise Knoizen and Kinnear, his roommate and an officer destined to become a four-star admiral, were making a simulated,

Skyraiders fly beneath the weather. One of the Able Dog's best features was its ability to travel long distances at low level below a potential enemy's radar to deliver a weapon on strategic targets. The AD was the first single-engine aircraft in the Navy to carry a special (atomic) weapon. Ed Heinemann and his group worked on the design requirements, and R. G. Smith made numerous drawings of the installation details prior to test flights in 1951.

low-level strike run on Hiroshima. U.S. Air Force planes were to act as the opposing force. "They were supposed to get us before we reached the target," recalled Knoizen. "The weather was a little less than horrible that day. When Gus, who was leading, and I reached the coast we ducked underneath the clouds, leveled off at 100 feet, found a railroad track, and barreled down it all the way to Hiroshima. When we reached the target, Gus clicked his mike and for the benefit of Air Force ears reported, 'We're here. Bang, bang. You're dead.'"

Said Knoizen, "I led the return leg and aligned us on the railroad. Somebody must have thrown a switch or something because after a time the track suddenly stopped, and we were confronted by the

unsettling spectre of a box canyon. We went Max Bendix [full power] and climbed, damn near nipping the treetops. We kept up a frantic chatter trying to help each other, and escaped from the trap. We made it home none the worse for wear. The Air Force, by the way, didn't like the weather that day and never got off the ground.''

Torque is defined as something that produces or tends to produce a torsion or rotation. It is a twisting, or wrenching, effect, or moment, exerted on a body by a force acting at a distance. In simpler terms, torque is what took place whenever power was added to the Wright R-3350 engine that drove the Skyraider. The nose of the aircraft was actually pulled or forced to the left. Rotational prop wash on the vertical tail also was a factor. Pilots had to counteract this motion with substantial right rudder, especially on takeoffs.

Grampaw Pettibone, the fictional sage of safety, knows all about torque. (Featured in *Naval Aviation News* magazine since World War II, the character is still drawn by the eminent artist and satirist Robert Osborn, with the narrative written by a naval officer.) Gramps' acerbic snaps at flyers are designed to help prevent mishaps, or at least have pilots and aircrews learn from those that have occurred. Responding to the report of a young flyer who had trouble during carrier qualifications in a Skyraider, he had something to say about the Skyraider and its notorious but manageable torque effect. The pilot mismanaged a deck run, let torque get the best of him, leaped from the deck in a near stall, lost control off the bow, stalled, and crashed. (Happily, however, he did survive.)

Railed Pettibone: ''Fetch me another aspirin tablet cause this one [accident report] made my port ulcer do nip-ups. This lad found out the hard way that the ole reliable Spad is like most of the birds we drive around in. You have to use a little influence on it sometime to make it go the way you want it to. You just can't sit there and let the cantankerous beast have its head without getting into more trouble than most people can handle. This lad made old Gramps' list but its not the one you brag about.''

An AD-4N was in the landing pattern for a night recovery on a carrier. In its aft compartment were the aircrewmen, a crusty chief petty officer, and a young sailor. While on the upwind turn, the Skyraider for some reason smacked into the water and began to submerge.

''No sweat,'' said the experienced CPO to his charge in the darkened compartment. ''The jolt you just felt was the shock of catching the arresting cable." The youthful technician wasn't so sure. "I hope you're right, Chief," he said, "but my feet are getting wet."

Whereupon the two men heard frantic beating on the fuselage access door. It was the pilot standing on the wing signaling them to get out. Indeed, the aircraft was in the water and sinking. Whether or not that sailor ever believed a chief again is not a matter of record.

One day a pilot was briefing his crewmen concerning emergency procedures in the AD-4N. "Now if you see me go by the window, that's your signal to bail out."

"Yes sir," said one of the radar operators. "But since we fly a lot at night, how are we going to tell?"

Perplexed, the pilot didn't have a proper answer, but the case was brought before the Douglas people. Consequently, a lanyard was installed near the pilot's headrest. During emergency egress the pilot was supposed to pull it, thereby ringing a bell in the crew compartment. When the crewmen heard that bell, they were to assume that the front end of the Skyraider was no longer occupied.

Hank Suerstedt, AD project officer at the time, amplified the story of the bail-out bell. He said "One of the crewmen's major worries in World War II TBMs during combat was how they would know whether or not to bail out if the pilot was incapacitated or killed. At BuAer we decided to put a warning bell in AD-4Ns and Ws. A spring-loaded machanism caused the bell to clang when manually actuated. The system also featured a red metal spring-loaded flag which popped into sight as a visual signal to the crew to bail out. Unfortunately, the bell was virtually inaudible in the back seats with the engine running and helmets on. Also, frequently on a catapult shot, the red flag popped out and nobody noticed it until later, causing much terror and confusion. Result: forget it!"

One amazing demonstration of the AD's inherent strength and "fly-ability" took place during qualification landings aboard a carrier off the California coast in the early 1950s. The pilot took the cut, chopped his throttle, and adjusted the aircraft's nose attitude for landing. But as the plane struck the deck, the tail hook skipped over the waiting cables.

On the straight-deck carriers, barriers were rigged at the end of the landing area to protect aircraft parked on the bow. Seeing those barriers after the "hook skip," the startled pilot pulled the control stick sharply toward his lap. The Skyraider ballooned clumsily over the obstacles, only to have the tail hook finally catch —on the top cable of the number three barrier. The AD was "thrown" into the ship's island structure and careened to the deck, skidding wildly on its left wheel.

Fearing he would be unable to stay on deck, the pilot added full power, and somehow was able to take off and fly away from the ship. The Air Boss then ordered him to proceed to North Island. Accompanied by a wingman, he did so and landed at the California base without further damage. About five feet of his starboard wing had been sheared off. The aileron was torn from its outboard hinge mounting and had streamed aft while airborne. Yet the Skyraider and its human cargo survived.

In the mid-1950s, as the cold war set people to thinking about nuclear attacks, naval aviation spent considerable time developing methods of delivering nuclear weapons to distant targets. Even though strategic planners in some quarters would have preferred all-jet air groups, the Skyraider could not be written off. In fact, the attack bomber became one of the foremost nuclear-capable airplanes. Pilots practiced low-level navigation flights (later called "Sandblowers") extensively, preparing themselves for the day everyone hoped would never come—that day when they might have to transport a bomb beneath the eyes of enemy radar over tremendous distances, at treetop height and below, and deliver it.

Pilots had to master techniques of navigation from near ground-level perspective, traveling at speeds of 160 knots and greater. Flying at altitudes of 200 feet and less, pilots had to compensate for what seemed to be distorted views of the land or sea, compared to what they were used to seeing several thousand feet above the earth. They often spent as many, if not more, hours planning a Sandblower as the number required to fly it. Large-scale maps that had to be cut and pasted together to create strip charts were mandatory. Prior to a low-level strike exercise, pilots convened in the air intelligence spaces on board the carrier with maps, scissors, paste, and colored pens to lay out designated routes, identify key landmarks— natural and man-made—along the way, and produce a portfolio complete with times and distances between check points. Skyraider pilots often needed several kneeboard cards for a single flight, so many were the check points along the way.

While some hops may have occupied six to eight hours in the air, others lasted a butt-busting dozen hours, or more. It was strenuous and painful work. Yet it was also immensely enjoyable flying. For some, the Sandblowers represented their best and most memorable hours in aviation.

Why? Because, in simple terms, Sandblowers constituted legal flat-hatting. They satisfied the primordial instinct to show off a little, to evince power, to experience the sensation of speed without sweating a traffic ticket. There is nothing quite so invigorating as whizzing over the countryside, racing along a canyon river, or zipping by a town or two, knowing that startled heads are craning to watch you; and then increasing speed to highball it on the final leg to the target, culminating the approach with a gut-wrenching, high-G (gravitational force) idiot loop (one-half cuban eight—a three-quarter loop followed by an upright recovery opposite to the run-in course), in order to "toss" the weapon and escape safely from its concussive effects; and then descending again for the long trip back to ship or home field.

Because of their unusually long duration and the challenge to dead-reckoning skills (direction-finding equipment didn't function well below 200 feet), these strikes, as flown by Skyraider pilots, distinguished those men from all other combat flyers. Not that jet drivers didn't fly Sandblowers —they did. But no one else had to endure the posterior misery and brain-numbing discomfort that plagued the Skyraider pilot's anatomy as he sat in one spot, without relief, for periods that often exceeded an eight-hour working day. The jet Sandblowers didn't last that long except under unusual circumstances, whereas AD pilots performed these flights with some regularity.

An airborne meal on one of these excursions might consist of a ham sandwich or two, warm pineapple juice, a candy bar, and an apple. A canteen of water was available but was usually too warm to be refreshing; rather, it merely slaked the thirst. If you smoked, by the time you got back from a marathon run, your throat felt like the Sahara at noon. Incidentally, the AD cockpit featured a crucial relief tube, without which a Sandblower could become an exercise in agony. On more than one occasion a Skyraider pilot, for some reason or other, angered a member of the maintenance department enough to inspire retaliation. Stuffing up the relief tube, especially before an eight-hour-plus low-level, was an exquisite way to get revenge.

VX-3 (the X representing "experimental") conducted two series of test flights under the cognizance of the Navy's Operational Development Force in 1951 and 1952. They were staged out of Naval Air Station Atlantic City and employed the Putnam target complex twenty-five miles south of Jacksonville, Florida. Twenty-five pilots and five aircrewmen, in AD-4s and AD-4Qs, flew across the eastern seaboard to Putnam and returned, nonstop, staying at 200 feet

Skyraider

above the terrain most of the way. Each aircraft carried three external fuel tanks. Sorties averaged a burdensome 11.1 hours each.

Thirty-four pilots and four aircrewmen participated in the second series of tests. Some of these flights lasted 13.5 hours!

Flight surgeons and other officials asked the returning flyers a battery of questions. How did weather affect them? Was their clothing comfortable? How much food did they consume? What was their liquid intake? Were there significant navigational problems? Did the aircraft and its equipment function as advertised? Were they confronted by psychogenic problems? How was their landing proficiency after such a debilitating time airborne? It would a be a shame to go all that way and then crash at the finish because of fatigue or some other dilemma.

In addition to the overall discomfort and the stress that attended the relentless requirement to navigate all the way, pilots had to monitor fuel consumption. The flow of gas from external tanks was controlled manually by an on–off handle on the port console in the cockpit, but there were no fuel-quantity gages for the external tanks, so timing their depletion was up to the pilot. At low altitude, should a tank run dry, he had to shift to another immediately, or the engine would stop and not begin again until gas was fed to the eighteen cylinders. The Skyraider, in the meantime, was a glider and could strike the ground in short order without prompt corrective action.

The VX-3 study led to significant recommendations. Not all were adopted, and others were tried only to be discontinued. But if nothing else, VX-3 brought a new awareness to the trials and tribulations of low-level flying over long periods. Some of the recommendations included: use of aspirin for headaches; modification of the Mae West's collar to prevent chafing of the neck; lighter helmets; use of Dexedrine for night landings at the end of long flights; a modest use of Dramamine to prevent or assuage airsickness; a parachute seat with extra cushions to alleviate hemorrhoidal pain; and, in a statement that didn't necessarily please strategic planners at the higher echelons of command, a limit on the number of low-level flights. "Because of buttock soreness," the report said, "a period of 48 hours should elapse between flights." (Some resourceful flyers took it upon themselves to reduce such pain and purchased "donuts" —inner-tube type cushions used by pregnant women—to sit on. A surgical tube could be attached to the inflation valve for blowing up or deflating it, as desired.)

Sans propeller, Skyraider number 3,180, last of its kind, nears end of El Segundo assembly line, January 1957.

William I. Nyburg, Hank Suerstedt's pal and helper in the armor-plate episode, was a commander selectee and C.O. of VC-33 in the Mediterranean in the mid-1950s. He was scheduled to fly an AD-4N with a wingman in a "straight" AD-6 on a low-level strike from the USS *Midway*.

"I had two 300-gallon tanks of gas," remembered Nyburg, "one on the centerline station and one on the left wing pylon. The radome was on the right wing pylon so a 1,000 pound 'waterfill' bomb was installed on a right wing rack to ensure symmetrical distribution of weight for the takeoff. The aircraft weighed 22,000 pounds. It was 0400 and so black I felt I was inside a cow's belly.

"I sucked up the gear immediately after leaving the deck and released the waterfill intentionally—almost hitting a destroyer in the process, which could have ruined my day before it hardly began—and started on the mission."

The carrier was north of Palmero. While Nyburg had OMNI, a navigational aid that provided bearing, but not distance, to ground stations, his own charts were primary means of guidance. In the hours that followed the two planes passed through three full weather systems. Their track took them to the Gulf of Corinth, the Dardanelles, and then to the "target," an airfield in Istanbul, Turkey.

Said Nyburg, "The weather was such that we decided to approach the target from the east. We spotted a DC-3 headed for the field and followed it right on in. We performed our 'Truman Eight,' and began the leg to the second target, another airfield—this time in Athens, Greece." (The Truman Eight, named after President Truman, was the medium angle loft, or one-half cuban eight, "toss" mode for nuclear weapons delivery. In this case there was, of course, only "simulated" ordnance on board the plane. It was called the Truman Eight, by the way, because it was a "Harry S." maneuver.)

After Athens, the two pilots headed for the carrier which was now near Taranto at the end of the Italian boot. Frustratingly, about 100 miles from the flattop, Nyburg popped up, checked in, but was told not to come any closer for a while. A special exercise was in progress.

"I reduced power to 130 knots," said Nyburg, "and slowed the rpms to about 1,450. I could almost count the blades as they circled. Then we held . . . and held . . . and held, until cleared in. Let's just say I had a fuel gage reading of zero when I landed. My wingman was loaded. He had 100 pounds! When they measured my gas, they found 26 pounds. We had been airborne for more than 14 hours. We had to be helped out of the cockpit."

A junior officer from the squadron was at the foot of his plane as Nyburg was laboriously extricated from the aircraft. He'd been wearing an exposure suit, a cumbersome rubber affair that sealed the body from neck to toes.

"Skipper," said the young aviator, "you brought a record to *Midway* for time airborne. But I have a question to ask. How do you urinate in that poopy suit?"

"You do just that," said Nyburg, "you urinate *in* the suit." (The exposure suit could be loosened in the necessary places for access to the relief tube, but that was a real chore.)

The thermos of coffee and box lunch he carried were helpful to Nyburg. But he saved the medicinal brandy for a well-deserved post-flight reward. The flight surgeon came to see him in the ready room. "Did you use the medication?" he asked, referring to some stay-awake pills.

"No, I preferred not to," answered Nyburg, returning the tablets.

"Where's your brandy?" the doctor queried.

"I just now drank it," replied Nyburg.

"Why did you do that?" asked the physician. "It was for use on the flight, if necessary."

"Well," said Nyburg with a sigh, "you told me it was 'survival' medicine. I survived, so I drank it." End of conversation.

Nyburg did indeed survive and retired as a captain. He might agree with the assessment of another captain, Ted Wilbur, who remembers those low-levels. Wilbur, a former editor of *Naval Aviation News* and a well-known artist, likened the low-flying, heavy-payload-carrying Skyraider to today's cruise missile. Like the ADs the pilotless cruise missiles travel enormous distances close to the ground to avoid detection by enemy radar. But their rear ends never get sore.

Richard F. Albright was an eighteen-year-old assigned to the Aviation Fundamentals School, Naval Air Auxiliary Training Center, Norman, Oklahoma, in 1957. Having grown up on films like *A Wing and A Prayer*, *Men of the Fighting Lady*, *Flattop*, and *The Bridges of Toko Ri*, he anticipated with great relish his turn at firing up the R-3350 on an AD-2 used for aircraft familiarization training. He had carefully studied the starting procedures, an outline of which follows for readers who retain a sentimental attachment to the bird:

Check magneto switch in OFF position.
Set fuel selector valve to MAIN
Place fuel boost switch ON
    CAUTION: Before engaging starter or attempting to start engine, receive ALL CLEAR signal from man on ground.
Place MAG switch to BOTH
Depress starter switch
Prime intermittently while depressing starter switch
When engine fires and begins to run, move mixture control to
    NORMAL
Release starter switch
Turn fuel boost pump OFF
Check oil pressure
    CAUTION: Oil pressure must register within 10 seconds, and must reach 40 psi (pounds per square inch) within 30 seconds.

"After a day or so in the classroom, the company marched over to the aircraft," said Albright. "One by one we climbed into the cockpit via the port wing and started her up. After a sixty-second run-up we were supposed to dismount via the starboard wing so that the next sailor could have a try."

Savoring the moment, Albright got in and started the engine, which purred quickly to life. The sixty seconds passed all too fast. When the chief petty officer in charge signaled him to shut down and get out, Albright stayed.

"I wasn't about to cut the engine before overdosing on the prop-wash and AVGAS (aviation gas) fumes whipping back along both sides of the AD-2," he said. "The chief nearly had to pull a .45 to get me out."

Later, on board the USS *Kearsarge*, Albright spent a lot of time on the after flight deck as a "plane pusher" in the V-1 Division. For him, "There couldn't have been a more exciting job in the peacetime Navy." The ADs were parked in the "pack," aft. Night ops with the AD-5Ns especially intrigued him.

He recalled, "I preferred the last row in the pack of 20 or more planes, all turning up at the same time. We were turned into the wind, and that, combined with the propwash of all those Skyraiders, sent splinters and debris from the deck whizzing back at us like miniature shrapnel. All we could see were the flashlight wands of the plane directors and the winking blue exhuast flames licking back from the cowl flaps. Like a roller coaster ride, it was a terror and a joy at the same time. You gripped your wheel chock with one hand and groped for a pad-eye with the other, all the time hoping you wouldn't be blown over the side and out of sight. Finally, the last AD would roar aloft, and you could laze about until recovery time. Daytime air operations weren't even in the same ballpark.

"My only bad memory of the Guppy model is that the huge radar pod under the fuselage made it impossible to tell if the port chock-man was still at his post or already ducking into the catwalk. I later became a sound-powered phone talker in Primary Fly Control and no longer had to worry about chock-men, port or starboard."

Unsubstantiated is the story of another young man who was devoted, in a different way, to the Skyraider. As the story goes, an AD crashed into a lake in upstate New York. Naval officials said that the aircraft could not be salvaged, and it was left at the bottom. But less than a month later, a young fellow told the Navy he thought he could retrieve the machine. Would the Navy buy it back? This was in the late 1950s, and how much the Navy offered is subject to conjecture. But the man did, somehow, raise the Skyraider from the lake's bottom, got it on a barge, had it towed down the Hudson

River, and eventually saw that it was transported to the Naval Air Station, Quonset Point, Rhode Island.

While the author can't verify this story, Commander Cliff Ruthrauff, a highly experienced naval aviator with considerable Skyraider time in his log book, flew an AD from Quonset Point to Oceana, Virginia, and it was, allegedly, the very same bird that had spent time in the New York lake.

Chief Petty Officer John G. Gourley, an ABFC (aviation boatswain mate—fueler) knows the Skyraider from rigorous times spent on board the USS *Lexington*, the USS *Yorktown*, and the USS *Shangri La*, in the early and mid-1960s.

"I may not be able to add any glamour to pilot stories or to those by the mechs who had to keep the old birds flying," said Gourley. "But I can tell you a small amount about the feelings of a flight deck crewman during Black-Out night operations, with a huge prop coming up the deck towards the waiting servicing crews on the starboard bow. Or when the wind was coming hard over the bow while trying to fuel the first plane there. There was nothing to hold onto, and the skin of the AD being cold and often wet, made for some pretty hairy moments."

Gourley continued, "Trying to ease a heavy brass nozzle off the wing, losing your footing and going to the deck with it, were always problems. Those drop tanks on the Skyraiders were so high at the fueling point that it was a strain to get the nozzle into them, and then to hold on and try to control the flow. The fumes that came from the tanks always got you a little light-headed no matter which way you turned to get away from them. The -Q and the -W models were my favorites. You could lay down on the wing, place your back to the wind, and listen to the tank for the sound that told you it was nearly full.

"When I think back to those days, I don't readily remember the F-8 Crusaders on the catapults, nor the clumsy F3H Demons coming up the deck. The first thought I have is of the blue flames shooting out from the exhaust on the ADs in the pre-dawn hours as they warmed up for launch."

And many are the mechs who remember, with chagrin, having to pull thirty-hour sump checks on Skyraiders parked on the "roof" —with twenty-five to thirty-five knots of wind blowing down the deck and oil splattered all over the machines, evoking from the sailors some of the most colorful commentaries ever hurled at the weather and at ship personnel, who, more often than not, couldn't

Skyraider

afford them space to do the job on the hangar deck.

For example, in the early 1960s aboard the *Forrestal*, VA-85 A-1s seldom went below for the check, which required an examination of the oil in the sump for signs of metal—a possible indication of engine problems. Skyraiders flew up thirty hours in a hurry; so sump checks were as common as they were unwieldly to perform.

A certain measure of jealousy developed on the part of the prop people, to whom, it seemed, hangar space was at a premium. When the ship's flight deck crew constructed a sort of portable shield consisting of a frame of two-by-fours with canvas walls to cut off the wind, that helped a little. But it would have been a whole lot easier to pull those sumps without having to fight the elements as well.

Like any airplane, the Skyraider was also part of some less than glorious adventures. In the early 1960s, for example, a couple of AD-5 pilots based at a West Coast air station launched eastward to an inland target for bombing and rocket-firing practice. The weather was excellent, but the number two man began to feel ill after the climb-out. He grew dizzy and was unable to properly hook up his oxygen mask. So he decided to land at a small civilian airfield that he spotted below on the desert floor. The leader watched the landing, got an "I'm OK" wave from the pilot, and went on to the target, where he expended his ordnance.

On his way home he stopped at the small strip to see his wingman, who was still woozy and not yet ready to fly. The leader took off, promising to send help. Back at the base he checked in with his C.O., who decided to visit the downed flyer himself, accompanied by the flight leader. The two set out for the desert strip in another AD-5. The sick pilot would be brought home by the C.O., and the flight leader would fly the other Skyraider home. Or so they planned.

Before they left, however, the operations duty officer at their field informed the aviators that the airport where the sick comrade waited wasn't on the list of approved landing sites for military aircraft. Undaunted, the duo decided to press on.

A while later they motored onto the desert strip. The sick flyer got into the C.O.'s bird while the flight leader manned the other aircraft and began taxiing downwind, on the runway, toward the takeoff point.

All of a sudden, about 600 feet from that point, his AD-5 seemed to settle. It was a most disquieting sensation. Then, abruptly, the aircraft nosed up. The weighty Able Dog had broken through the runway surface! Perhaps the ODO's warning should have been heeded.

Investigation revealed that the runway was only three-quarter-inch asphalt over rolled desert sand. OK for Piper Cubs maybe but not bigger machines like the Skyraider.

No one got airmanship awards for that episode.

The AD could adapt itself to most any type of mission, no matter how outlandish. It could lay smoke screens, drop chaff for ECM purposes, spray DDT, and even serve as a platform for delivering bean bags. An AD pilot on a Mediterranean carrier in 1961 or thereabouts was tasked with winging low over a surfaced submarine and tossing a bean bag onto it, simulating delivery of a strategically important message in a weighted satchel. It worked. He scored a direct hit.

At about the same time, a Hollywood producer got the Navy's agreement to help him make a movie about World War II. Propeller aircraft, like those flown in the 1940s, were needed in some scenes. Although the Skyraider had never served in that global conflict, it was piston-powered and available. So, caught in a sort of time warp, the Skyraider was selected. VA-85 A-1s, flying from the *Forrestal* in the Mediterranean, were the performers. For several days they swept over convoys, strafed beaches, and bombed strongholds. Unfortunately, however, only a few seconds of the many, many hours of Skyraider action survived the film editor's scissors.

Another undocumented tale has persisted through the years. It allegedly took place in the mid- or late 1960s in the Mediterranean. True or not, it's an amusing manifestation of the type of sea story that crops up when an airplane stays in the inventory as long as the Skyraider did.

Two A-1s launched north of Sicily for a patrol along the North African coast looking for a Soviet ship. They got themselves caught in some unexpectedly bad weather with severe winds and were blown drastically off course. Running low on fuel, they were forced to push over, go down through the clouds, and try to pinpoint their position. Apparently, they were having nav aid trouble as well.

To their surprise, when they broke clear, they found themselves over land, but whose land they didn't know. They ran out of gas and had to put down, gear up, on the unknown terrain. They might have been in Algeria or, perhaps, Libya. The first thing they saw was an Arab gentleman riding a camel.

At NAS Lemoore Skyraider retirement ceremony in April 1968, Lieutenant (Junior Grade) Ted Hill mans number 405, VA-25's and the Navy's last A-1H/J model Skyraider.

In short order the two intruders were taken into custody in a nearby city, and they were placed in a jail cell a story or two above ground level. During the night they climbed out of the cell using bed sheets they had tied together. Dressed in bright orange flight suits, they managed to get to the American embassy. When an embassy official realized what had happened, he knew he had a problem on his hands. Perhaps, relations between the United States and that country were less than ideal. Or, maybe the American official was concerned that his newly arrived constituents had violated the local law by breaking out of prison.

To avoid a potentially embarrassing incident he smuggled the naval aviators back *into* the jail. Next day, under more proper circumstances, he got them out legally. Meanwhile the natives had removed the twenty-millimeter cannons from the Skyraiders. The planes were eventually repaired by a team from the Navy and returned to U.S. custody.

Chief Warrant Officer James W. Doran was in VA-52 aboard the USS *Ticonderoga* between 1964 and 1966. The squadron flew A-1s in Vietnam. Its planes had funnel-shaped flash suppressors fitted to the muzzles of the twenty-millimeter cannons, and on one strafing run a little bird slammed into the flash suppressor on the starboard, inboard gun.

Said Doran, "When the pilot pulled the trigger, that gun opened up like a banana peel. After the aircraft returned to the ship three of us —myself, and Ordnancemen Glen D. Sanders and Carl M. Collier [both of whom became chief petty officers]—were told to remove the gun and turn it in for replacement. Approximately eight hours, twelve hack-saw blades, and six sore arms later, we'd finally cut the barrel off about four inches from the leading edge of the wing. After pulling the gun and carrying it into the shop we learned there were no spares in stock. We cleaned up the gun, now called 'Stubby' for obvious reasons, and reinstalled it in the aircraft. Needless to say, Stubby became the most accurate and maintenance-free gun in the squadron.

"In another incident, the carrier was low on bombs and preparing to rendezvous with an ammunition ship for replenishment when a strike was requested by a forward air controller over land. He had apparently found a North Vietnamese convoy on a mountain road and U.S. Air Force aircraft had it bottled up. *Tico* didn't have enough bombs for everybody, so the Tinkertoys [A-4 Skyhawks] launched with all that were available. The Spad drivers ended up with an ordnance load that I'd heard was possible but never seen: Mark 54 depth bombs fitted with AN/M-103A1 nose fuzes. According to stories I heard after the flight the convoy was totally destroyed, and the blast effect of the depth bombs did more damage than the general-purpose bombs delivered by the A-4s."

Continued Doran, "Then there was the time two shipmates, Ordnanceman Third Jim Freeman and Airman Parachute Rigger Bob Overcash, thought it would be great if the Navy had a parachute-retarded version of the Mark 76 practice bomb. [The carrier could tow a spar for practice bombing off the stern.] They proceeded to drill holes in the tail fins of one and to design and attach a small parachute, complete with an arming device, to open the chute upon release. The hardest part was to convince a Spad driver to drop it. After a thorough search they finally convinced Lieutenant A. D. 'Spad' Wilson to deliver the weapon.

"The device didn't work. The parachute got tangled up, streamed behind the bomb, and caused Wilson to miss the spar by about a quarter mile."

Doran also recalled, "One day the Chief told us to get rid of another Mark 76, one that had been laying around the shop for a few months. I can report that this practice bomb left the *Ticonderoga* as part of an Alpha strike against a North Vietnamese target. Three Spads launched, carrying two 500 pounders and a dozen 260-pound fragmentation bombs. The fourth took off with two 500 pounders, eleven 260-pound frags, and one Mark 76 practice bomb. Somewhere in North Vietnam a Communist ordnance disposal team is still trying to de-arm the only Mark 76 to be dropped in combat."

John C. Bowman was an aviation technician in VA-85 aboard the *Forrestal* during a 1962–1963 deployment. He loved the Skyraider, but there were times the machine drove him up the wall.

"I was often assigned to pull and replace black [electronic] boxes. Late one afternoon I was half in and half out of the hell hole of one of our birds trying to extract an ARC-27 radio set. The hell hole was small, the ARC-27 large. You get the picture. I'm cussing the thing because I couldn't get it out of its rack.

"Someone beat on the side of the plane," remembered Bowman. "I heard a voice ask something to the effect, 'What do you think of this aircraft you're working on?' At that particular instant I was in no mood to answer any questions. Frankly, I was about ready to roll that A-1 over the round down. I gave an answer keeping the expletives to a minimum, but there was no denying the angered frustration in my voice. In effect my words said, 'A piece of junk to work on, but the best plane we got, why?'"

Whereupon Bowman emerged from the hell hole. He said, "I turned around to see who was asking such a stupid question and came eyeball to eyeball with the crest on Admiral (John) Hyland's hat. He was Sixth Fleet commander. For a striker like me with less than a year in the Navy, this was quite an experience. I had never seen a real live admiral before. I was shaking in my boondockers and thought 'I guess I'll find out where the brig is.' I saluted and gave a poorly worded apology for the language I had used. Then the admiral said, 'That's quite all right, sailor. I asked for an opinion and got an honest one. Carry on.' With that he turned and walked toward the island with his Marine Corps guard in tow."

Bowman also remembered the time one of the squadron ensigns was bombing the spar towed behind the ship. "For some reason—as I recall the electrical problem blamed for the incident was dismissed by the electricians—the young pilot pickled his wing tanks instead of his Mark 76 practice bombs. The starboard tank, complete with fuel, scored a kill on the spar."

Continued Bowman, "Ever since my first encounter with the AD it has held a special place in my heart. I can remember how mad we all got when the weather grounded all the jets and the only planes aloft were the Spads. It wasn't the prettiest or the fastest aircraft around but absolutely was the most reliable weapons platform ever to fly.

"In 1980 I took my family to Patuxent River for their annual open house and air show. I arrived just as vintage war birds were arriving. The last one to come in was a Spad. I had to touch her. Although the display area was roped off, I managed to get permission from the owner to look closely at the plane. Everything came back. I managed to get my hands dirty from the oil that covered the sides; I remembered back to washing the blades with hydraulic fluid and putting them at attention after tying the machine down. I felt that I had renewed an old friendship. There was a large assortment of fine aircraft there that day: F-18s, F-14s, F-4s. But I spent most of my time hanging around that AD. On my way home I felt on top of the world."

In 1962 Ken Knoizen, the Korean veteran, was piloting AD-6s with the "Valions" of VA-15 in the Mediterranean aboard the USS *Roosevelt*. "I've always held the belief," he said, "that if there's a rainshower in the area, the carrier will get under it and stay there no matter what the rest of the world looks like. One evening with a bright moon overhead, a pair of A-4 Skyhawks, two of us in Skyraiders, and a single A-3 Skywarrior took off. My wingman was a young lieutenant nicknamed 'Crash.' He had had an untoward incident or two on previous flights. We completed our mission, returned to the ship, and, not surprisingly, found it bathing under a horrendous thunderbumper. I advised the ship that if it would move 15 miles in any direction, the weather was clear. I was succinctly informed that operations precluded diverting from the present course, which was apparently the same course as the storm. The Scooters (A-4s) entered the landing pattern, made two or three tries apiece, and got aboard. The huge Skywarrior made four passes before snagging a wire. The A-3 pilot's view was so obliterated by the heavy rain that

Rear Admiral Ken Knoizen.

he announced over the radio, 'If somebody will tell me where to go, I'll taxi out of the gear. At the moment I cannot see a single thing.'

"It was our turn next," said Knoizen. "I made my approach through waterfall-like rain that let up a bit at the ramp. I took the cut, brought the throttle back, overdid my dive for the deck, and boltered. I roared away for another turn. Crash, meanwhile, drove through a solid wall of water that seemed to have been conjured up by a demon from the deep. He was at the landing point, and the LSO issued him sharp directions: Cut! Power! Power! Wave off! S--t!'"

The right wing of Crash's AD dipped. Things turned to worms in a hurry. His aircraft struck three F-8 Crusaders parked to the right of the foul line, then floundered on up the deck smashing into more planes. A dozen aircraft were damaged, three or four of them beyond repair. Crash's AD ended up on the straight-deck portion of the ship atop an A-3.

"Oddly," said Knoizen, "we couldn't find Crash in the wreckage. After a while he was located in the ready room, huddled uncertainly in a chair."

Ironically, the catastrophe lit up the flight deck. "It made my landing easier," said Knoizen. "I was hurried out of the cockpit by the flight deck crew so that firefighting efforts could continue."

Knoizen was also a commander and C.O. of the VA-165 "Boomers" aboard the USS Coral Sea in the early days of the Vietnam War. (The ship was extended beyond its normal tour and didn't return to the United States until November 1965, after an eleven month cruise.) "Ours was the first squadron of any kind to drop a million pounds of bombs on the enemy," he said. "In fact we expended more than four and three-quarter million pounds of bombs, rockets and 20-millimeter on the deployment. We had a birthday cake to celebrate the one million milestone, and although it was rather macho, we used cluster bomblets as candles."

Continued Knoizen, "There was an island off the North Vietnamese coast which we were advised contained a major cache of ammunition. It became a target, and our air group met severe opposition during a subsequent attack. Four aircraft were lost, two Skyhawks and two Crusaders, but the pilots, two of whom were squadron C.O.s, survived. One of our Spad drivers scored a beautiful hit on a cave entrance. The explosion that followed made that one of Walt Clark's with a 2,000 pounder in Korea seem like a bonfire. The whole island erupted, like Krakatoa, East of Java. I'm told the explosions continued sporadically for days. The flyers in the water were retrieved that day except for the F-8 squadron skipper, Commander Bill Donnely. A dozen of our Spads covered the waterfront looking for him for two days. We were too far south, however, and it wasn't until the third day that we found him well to the north. During his perilous hours in a survival raft a Chinese destroyer came into view. He wisely went into the water and hid beneath his upturned raft. A helicopter finally hauled him to safety."

When a naval A-6 Intruder was shot down west of Hanoi, a major rescue operation ensued. Knoizen's Spads launched at 0400, not to return until hours later, at 2200. There were eight planes involved; four at a time conducted searches for the downed crewmen, while the other four waited at the U.S. Air Force base in Udorn, Thailand. After one eight-hour shift per group the ADs returned to the *Coral Sea*. Another aircraft with a two-man crew had gone down in the same vicinity, and Knoizen observed, "We had the whole nine yards going for a while—helicopters, our Spads, an Air Force C-130. Two of the four downed flyers were saved."

On another matter, Knoizen recalled an unusual experiment conducted at the suggestion of the carrier division commander, Rear Admiral Edward Outlaw. "He wanted to see if depth charges, de-

Skyraider

signed for use at sea, could penetrate the thick jungle and detonate with effect," said Knoizen. "Four of our Spads launched with a load of the blunt-edged weapons, staggered into the sky, and proceeded to a thickly carpeted jungle area. We released the charges, they disappeared beneath the foliage, and the explosions were apparently so muffled by the jungle that they were ineffective. That was the only time we used depth charges over land."

Continued Knoizen, "I'm proud of the fact that we lost only one pilot in VA-165. It could have been much worse. Jim Parrie was my wingman one day and took a hit while bombing in Laos that produced a hole big enough to crawl through. But the Skyraider got him home. In fact, even with the Korean experience behind me, my respect and admiration for the A-1 grew in Vietnam. Lieutenant Marty Demko came back one day with 260 holes in his machine. He had no hydraulics, and no radio, but that R-3350 kept on turning.

"In retrospect, although I'm certainly prejudiced, I believe the Skyraider was the greatest flying machine ever built. Not only was it a superlative performer in combat. It was the last of the fun airplanes.

"It was also the vehicle for unbelievable heroics by some extraordinary pilots," said Knoizen. "One naval aviator in particular comes to mind, Commander (later Rear Admiral) Gordon Smith, Jr., skipper of VA-52. Apart from having to bail out of his damaged Spad *upside down* over the water one dark night, which is one type of heroic effort, he was the kind of guy who just wouldn't quit on a rescap.

"I don't recall the details, but some flyers had been shot down following a raid over North Vietnam. A rescue effort was under way. Gordon hung in there helping out until he absolutely had to leave because of dwindling fuel. In fact his carrier turned on the knots and sped northward to intercept him as he was coming south, so precarious was the situation. He snagged a wire just as he ran out of gas. I repeat, he was a guy who wouldn't quit. In a way, I feel the Skyraider itself was like that, too."

As the 1960s drew to a close and the days of the Skyraider passed inevitably toward a final sunset, a phenomenon of sorts developed. It came on slowly and steadily, like a London fog, and spread throughout the fleet and shore stations around the globe. In their own way, people in the world of aviation began saying a long goodbye to the Skyraider. It seemed that no other aircraft in the autumn of its life had ever evoked such across-the-board praise. Much of the adulation carried the friendly nip of humor.

"Jets Are For Kids" was stenciled on the helmets of plane captains aboard the USS *Kennedy*, a tribute to the EA-1s of the carrier's VAQ-33, Det 67. Above the word NAVY on the fuselage of one of the birds was a reference to antiquity: "ON LEASE FROM THE SMITHSONIAN INSTITUTE."

Lieutenant (Junior Grade) Ernie Massa, a naval flight officer in Det 67, was proud to be among the last of the Navy's Spad crews. It was 1969 when he said, "Hell, everybody drives a '66 Ford, but how many Model 'Ts' do you see on the road?"

"What's it like to fly?" was a common question asked of A-1 pilots, especially by younger folk, near the end. A common answer was: "If you treat it right, it'll treat you right. And it should never be taken for granted."

Airman Second Class Ronald L. Gregory of the U.S. Air Force worked on A-1s in Vietnam. He wrote the editor of *Airman*, an official publication:

> Sir: You recently carried in your magazine four pages about the F-100 in Vietnam. The A-1Es carry more weight on one wing than the F-100s on both. We have carried more weight in one bomb (2,000 pounds) than the F-100 does all the way across. Members of Army ground units have written many letters of thanks for the air support the A-1E has given them in time of need. Ask the Army or Marine foot soldier which is the number one support plane here. They will answer the A-1E. Both the pilots and ground crews of the 633rd Combat Support Group are doing an outstanding job. They deserve more credit than they've been given. And please don't ever refer to the A-1E as a sputtering prop-driven aircraft. It doesn't sputter—it purrs and sounds so sweet to the rifleman's ears.

"From bullets to bombs to electrons—the A-1 had it all," penned a professional observer. Another declared that "A Spad driver flies a plane that is much older than its jet cohorts. He can't climb as high, cruise as fast, or dive as quickly, so he must compensate with superb airmanship." The MiG shoot-downs in Vietnam are testimony to that.

South Vietnamese pilots became superb airmen in the Spad as well. They respected the aircraft dearly although some called it *trau dien*, which means "crazy water buffalo."

In a display of profound respect, *Naval Aviation News* magazine, which has been covering events since World War I, gave the A-1 the longest feature ever to appear in the publication until that time (July 1968).

Few combat airplanes have left their mark in so many places around the earth. Elsewhere in this book there are stories of ADs that made forced landings in Greece, Turkey, and North Africa, but were saved to fly another day. There was also Ensign P. S. Gallegos back in the 1950s. He ran into a wayward bird and put his Skyraider down, wheels up, in a muddy potato patch in Denmark. Cursed as the journey was, a persevering group of American and Danish Army personnel moved that aircraft more than 100 miles so that it could be fixed and flown again.

There was a spirit of determination, a determination to get the job done, solidly imbued in the Skyraider. Somehow, inexplicably perhaps, that spirit became contagious. The human beings exposed to the A-1—the designers, pilots, aircrewmen, maintenance men, buffs, and even the Danish soldiers who had to haul one out of a muddy potato patch—caught it.

That spirit was embodied in the aviator who rolled in high and called into focus every nuance of his bombing skills so that he could drop a bridge or put a 500 pounder precisely on target close to the front lines, careful not to harm friendly troops.

It was embodied in the radar and ECM operators who patiently and laboriously, hour after hour, scanned the scopes and operated the gear that gave the Skyraider new dimensions of tactical value for the entire fleet.

It was embodied in the pilot who was "Winchester"—ammo gone, but who pressed on, buzzing the forest at perilously low heights to hold an enemy at bay so that a fellow flyer might be rescued.

It was embodied in the figure of a Skyraider pilot, Sandblower-bound, making his way across the flight deck, laden with plotting board, nav bag, helmet, pistol, flashlight, survival gear, box lunch—and an inner tube to ease the sure-to-come posterior pain.

It was embodied in the troops who fueled the tanks, armed the guns, hoisted the bombs, and kept the machine running in the heat of Asia or the cold of Korea.

It was embodied in the plane captains, heavy tie-down chains draped over tired shoulders, chocks held in scarred hands, as they waited for the birds to come home.

It was embodied in the genuinely forlorn expression of Lieutenant Commander (later Captain) Ralph Smith, a VA-25 pilot with more than 2,400 airborne hours behind that R-3350 engine. He was reflecting on the demise of the Skyraider. He sighed, "You know, I sort of feel like the Indian and the buffalo. I can see the sun going down."

It was embodied in the relentless devotion to A-1E, Bureau Number 135178, of naval aviator Jim Fausz. A flight instructor at Naval

Air Station Saufley Field, Pensacola, one day in 1969 he saw old 178, which had been sitting idle. He manipulated his way into flying it exclusively for the Naval Aviation Medical Institute as a medical research aircraft. For a while he could only do so nights and weekends because of primary duties. Eventually, however, it became a full-time assignment, and Fausz logged a memorable 500 hours in the aircraft before age, lack of parts, and official orders ended the idyll.

In a sequence of events that could themselves occupy a volume, Fausz kept track of 178 and after retiring from the Navy ferried it to Atlanta, Georgia, to its new owner. It's a safe bet Jim Fausz is still keeping a a devoted, if distant eye on that Spad.

When Rear Admiral David Welsh unveiled a display featuring a jet-powered A-4 Skyhawk during ceremonies at Naval Air Station Lemoore, California, prop-driven Skyraiders nearly stole the show. A large crowd was on hand at the dedication of "Welsh Park," in the administration area of the master jet base. Ed Heinemann, who also designed the A-4, was there along with Bob Rahn, Douglas Aircraft test pilot who had flown the A-1 extensively, and other VIPs.

While onlookers marveled at the jet on a pedestal, four Skyraiders swooped by unexpectedly. They were very low and very loud, their engines rumbling mightily. A cloud of leaflets blossomed in the sky and floated to the ground. The message on the leaflets was straight-forward enough:

WE'D RATHER FIGHT THAN SWITCH!

So it went in the final years of this superlative warplane. The Fists of the Fleet, VA-25, surrendered the last carrier-based A-1H/J in 1968. The U.S. and South Vietnamese Air Forces continued to fly Skyraiders in combat, and a naval A-1E variant here and there lingered in the inventory for a while. Nowadays, some of the Spads rest in storage in the sunlit comfort of a desert in the American Southwest. A few are in private hands and, happily, make occasional appearances at air shows across the land.

Long after the last of the last A-1s makes its final touch down, the Skyraider will be remembered. For above all else, it was a tough and enduring airplane that served its country well in war and peace.

During "cross-deck" operations an 849 Squadron AEW.1 lands aboard the USS *Essex* in 1959. (Fleet Air Arm Museum—Terry Treadwell)

The Royal Navy AD-4Ws were designated AEW.1s and flew with the British for a decade.

A

Summary of British, French, and Swedish Use of the Skyraider

In addition to the United States and South Vietnam, several other countries operated the Skyraiders, the principal ones being Great Britain, France, and Sweden. Britain, under the Mutual Defense Aid Program, was the first to get them. In November 1951 four of a total of 50 AD-4Ws arrived at Glasgow, Scotland, and were turned over to the Royal Navy.

The planes, which featured the APS-20 search radar and accommodations for a pilot plus two aircrewmen in the fuselage cabin, were redesignated AEW.1s. Their primary mission was to provide airborne early warning services for the fleet, particularly against low-flying aircraft. The Royal Navy's 778 Squadron, formed a month before receipt of the Skyraiders, was to evaluate U.S. electronic equipment. The Royal Navy's intent with the AEW.1s was to operate them as airborne radar platforms capable of controlling carrier air patrols and directing strike aircraft, in addition to the basic requirement of detecting targets at long range.

When 778 Squadron became a front-line unit in the summer of 1952, it was redesignated 849 Squadron. The balance of the fifty Skyraiders arrived for duty over the next couple of years. The planes wore a sea-blue gloss finish called "midnight blue." Four white lines in parallel on the port side of the vertical stabilizer were used as a guide for ground observers to a determine if the aircraft was in the proper attitude for landing.

The British operated the AEW.1s much like their U.S. naval

Skyraider

counterparts. A headquarters group remained ashore while operational "flights," or detachments of four aircraft each, deployed with Royal Navy carriers. In their nearly twelve-year tour with the British, the midnight-blue Skyraiders were mainstays of the carriers HMSs *Albion, Ark Royal, Bulwark, Centaur, Eagle,* and *Victorious.* As such they appeared in a wide variety of areas around the globe.

Number 849 Squadron, incidentally, was the first AEW unit in the Royal Navy, and the Skyraider was the last piston-engine aircraft, with the exception of helicopters, to serve with the Fleet Air Arm. At 25,000 pounds loaded, the AEW.1 was also one of the heaviest aircraft to serve in the Royal Navy. Its 3,000-mile range also rated among the top in capabilities.

When the AEW.1s passed from front-line service in 1960, they were replaced by the turbo-prop-driven Fairey AEW.3 Gannet. Whereas the Royal Navy aviators and aircrewmen highly praised the Douglas aircraft for its flying characteristics, British ground soldiers during the Suez campaign in the mid-1950s liked it for another reason. It was discovered that by removing one of the observer's seats in the fuselage cabin, more than 1,000 cans of beer could be stowed for delivery to troops on the beaches.

AEW.1 makes deck run.

Royal Navy Skyraider approaches carrier, wheels down, hook down. (Fleet Air Arm Museum—Terry Treadwell)

In the late 1950s France's Armée de l'Air needed a proven ground-attack and counter-insurgency plane to serve in the government's conflict with rebels in Algeria. Republic F-47D Thunderbolts had been used by the 20 Escadre. About a hundred ADs from surplus in America were turned over to the French to replace them beginning in 1960. Half or so were AD-4NAs; the others, AD-4Ns. The AD-4Ns were updated to qualify as AD-4NAs.

The aircraft were flown against the Front de Liberation Nationale—the FLN. Algeria, nonetheless, won its independence in 1962. The Skyraiders were later operated by Escadrons in the French territory of Afars and Issas (French Somaliland), and the Malagasy Republic. A few were turned over to the Republic of Chad and the Central African Republic. The aircraft were in limited service with the Armée de l'Air through the early 1970s, some even engaging in combat in 1970 against Muslim guerillas in the Republic of Chad's northern sector.

In a controversial move, France gave ten Skyraiders to Cambodia (now Democratic Kampuchea) in 1965. Five more AD-4NAs arrived

AEW.1 makes a trap. (Fleet Air Arm Museum—Terry Treadwell)

AEW.1s in formation.

later. These planes weren't used much until the government of Prince Norodum Sihanouk fell in 1970. After that they were flown against the Vietcong and North Vietnamese. Sabotage, ground fire, lack of training and qualified personnel led to the demise of this air force.

The Skyraider was the last piston-engine combat aircraft in the Armée de l'Air, a few remaining in service as late as 1974. One report showed the French to have logged 105,000 flight hours in the aircraft since receiving them in 1960. To be sure, it was a popular flying machine for them. One writer declared that the Skyraider had "plenty of poke . . . [and that it was] at the same time a Ferrari and a Rolls-Royce, and also a bulldozer."

In 1962 and 1963 a dozen of the Royal Navy's AEW.1s were sold to Sweden for use by the military as target-towing aircraft. The Scottish Aviation company of Prestwick, Scotland, refurbished the planes. Radomes, tail hooks, and the vertical fins on the horizontal stabilizer were removed. A large observation bubble, or window, was added on either side of the fuselage behind the fuselage access door. A winch operator's station was incorporated in the aircrew compartment.

As target-tugs for the Swedish Armed Forces, the Skyraiders were painted yellow with black registration markings. They towed three types of targets: the "strut" for army and naval air defense training; and the "wing" and the "arrow" for air force gunnery practice.

Skyraider Performance Data

Length	
AD-1, 2, 3	38′4″
AD-4, 6, 7	38′10″
AD-5	40′0″
Height	
AD-1, 2, 3	15′5″
AD-4, 5, 6, 7	15′8″
Wing span	50′0″
Engine	Wright R-3350
Maximum speed	300 + kts.
Service ceiling	27,000 + ft.
Combat range	1,100 + nm.
Payload	8,000 lbs.

Armament

AD-1, 2, 3 — Two 20mm guns, bombs, rockets, torpedoes carried externally.

AD-4, 5, 6, 7 — Four 20mm guns and increased external stores capacity.

Specification

Highlights; Basic Differences Between Models;
Main Versions

BT2D-1

AD-1 Versions: -1Q, electronic countermeasures; -1W, early warning; -1P, photo-reconnaissance; two 20 mm cannons

AD-2 Heavier than AD-1; strengthened inner wing; wheel well covers; increased fuel capacity; appeared in -2Q version.

AD-3 More structural strengthening; improved propeller; modified landing gear; redesigned canopy; -3N (night); -3Q; -3W; two -3S and two -3E versions with special submarine attack and search gear, respectively, for combined hunter-killer operations.

AD-4   Built in larger numbers than other models (1,051); improved radar, P-1 autopilot; -4B version was strengthened for toss and over-the-shoulder bombing with tactical nuclear weapons; four cannons; -4N; -4Q; -4W; -4L (winterized with anti-icing and de-icing equipment); -4NA; (stripped -4N for day attack); -4NL (also winterized).

AD-5   Side by side seating; widened forward fuselage; two feet longer than predecessors; larger vertical fin; deletion of dive brakes from sides of fuselage; multi-mission capability: combined ASW hunter-killer, transport, ambulance, photo-reconnaissance, target-towing; -5N; -5W; -5Q.

AD-6   Low-level bombing capability—basically, an improved AD-4B.

AD-7   Strengthened wings, landing gear and engine mounts.

Note: When U.S. military aircraft were redesignated in 1962, AD-4NA became A-1D, AD-5 – A-1E, AD-5W – EA-1E, AD-5Q – EA-1F; AD-5N = A-1G; AD-6 = A-1H; AD-7 = A-1J.

Total of 3,180 built.

For full details on Skyraider aircraft see bibliography and especially *McDonnell Douglas Aircraft Since 1920* by Rene J. Francillon, Putnam, London.

Totals Built and Bureau Numbers by Model

XBT2D-1: 25, Bu. Nos. 09085–09109.

AD-1: 242, Bu. Nos. 09110–09351; **AD-1Q:** 35, Bu. Nos. 09352–09386.

AD-2: 156, Bu. Nos. 122210–122365; **AD-2Q:** 22, Bu. Nos. 122366–122387

AD-3: 125, Bu. Nos. 122729-122853; **AD-3Q:** 23, Bu. Nos. 122854–122876; **AD-3W:** 31, Bu. Nos. 122877–122907; **AD-3N:** 15, Bu. Nos. 122908–122922.

AD-4: 372, Bu. Nos. 123771–124006, 127844–127879, 128917–129016; **AD-4N:** 307, Bu. Nos. 124128–124156, 124725–124760, 125707–125764, 126876–127018, 127880–127920; **AD-4W:** 168, Bu. Nos. 124076–124127, 124761–124777, 125765–125782, 126836–126875, 127921–127961; **AD-4Q:** 39, Bu. Nos. 124037–124075; **AD-4B:** 165, Bu. Nos. 132227–132391.

AD-5: 212, Bu. Nos. 132478, 132392–132476, 132637–132686, 133854–133929; **AD-5N:** 239, Bu. Nos. 132477, 132480–132636, 134974–135054; **AD-5W:** 218, Bu. Nos. 132729, 132730–132792, 133757–133776, 135139–135222, 139556–139605; **AD-5S:** 1, Bu. No. 132479.

AD-6: 713, Bu. Nos. 134466–134537, 135223–135406, 137492–137632, 139606–139821.

AD-7: 72, Bu. Nos. 142010-142081.

AD SPECIFICATIONS

VERSIONS	ENGINE WRIGHT R-3350	DIMENSIONS			WEIGHTS			PERFORMANCE		
		Span	Length	Height	Empty	Design Gross	Over Load	Max.	Service Ceiling	Combat Range
		ft.	ft.	ft.	lb.	lb.	lb.	k.	ft.	n.m.
Day Attack:										
XBT2D-1	24W	50	39.5	12	10,500	15,000	16,700	325	26,000	1,350
AD-1	24W	50	38.5	12	10,560	16,000	18,000	310	26,000	1,350
AD-2	26W	50	38.5	12	10,579	16,000	18,300	328	27,500	1,386
AD-3	26W	50	38.5	12	10,800	16,000	18,300	325	27,000	1,300
AD-4	26WA	50	38.5	12	11,712	16,700	24,000	315	36,500	1,110
AD-5	26WA	50	40	13.9	12,293	17,000	25,000	270	26,000	1,044
AD-6	26WA	50	39.2	12	11,302	15,600	25,000	285	28,500	1,143
AD-7	26WB	50	39.2	12	12,094	15,600	25,000	285	28,200	1,128
All-Weather:										
AD-3N	26W	50	38.5	12	11,564	17,000	18,300	315	26,500	1,300
AD-4N	26WA	50	38.5	12	11,400	17,400	24,000	305	36,000	1,100
AD-5N	26WA	50	40	13.9	12,112	17,000	25,000	260	25,000	1,135
Countermeasure:										
AD-1Q	24W	50	38.5	12	10,970	17,000	18,900	300	24,500	1,250
AD-2Q	26W	50	38.5	12	11,200	17,000	19,143	321	26,600	1,301
AD-3Q	26W	50	38.5	12	11,600	17,000	18,300	305	36,000	1,100
AD-4Q	26WA	50	38.5	12	11,600	17,000	24,000	305	36,000	1,100
AD-5Q	26WA	50	40	13.9	12,097	17,000	25,000	270	27,000	1,182
Airborne Early Warning:										
AD-3W	26W	50	38.5	12	13,000	16,500	18,300	300	27,000	1,300
AD-4W	26WA	50	38.5	12	12,600	17,500	24,000	305	36,000	1,100
AD-5W	26WA	50	40	13.9	12,092	17,000	25,000	260	27,000	1,294

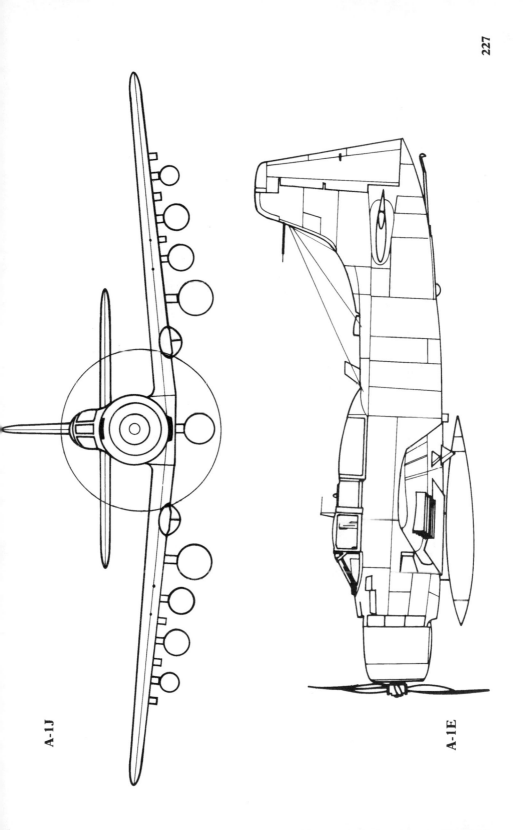

A-1J

A-1E

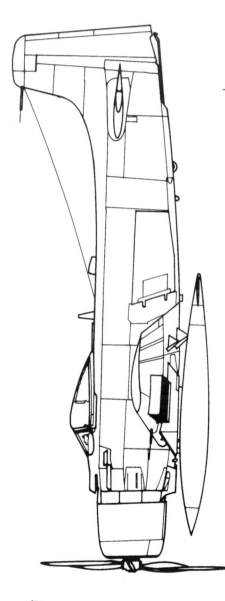

A-1J

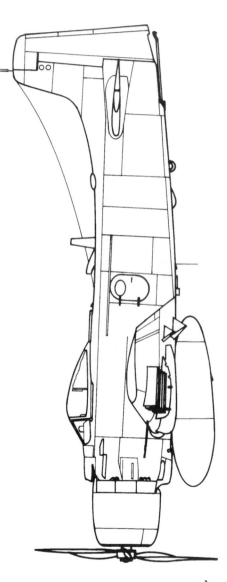

AD-4NL

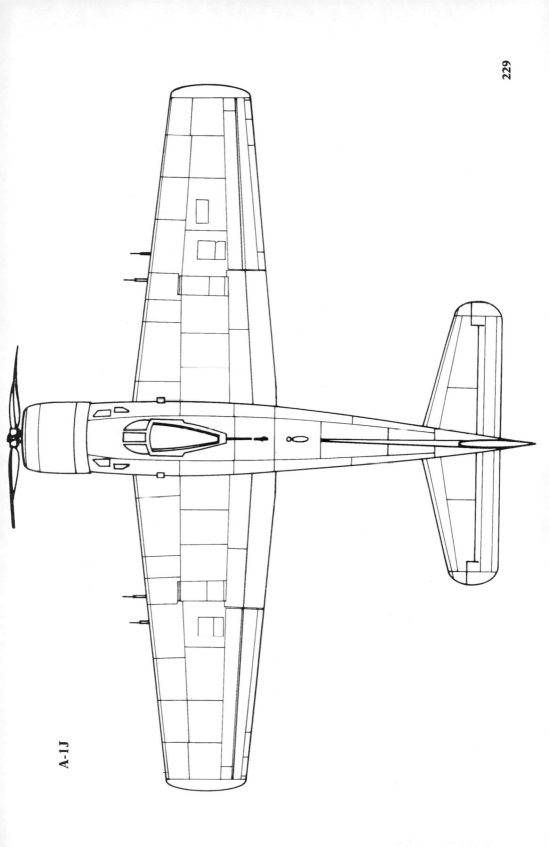

A-1J

Maintenance Areas of the A-1E

1. Tail Control Surface Linkage
2. Tail Wheel Installation
3. Electronics
4. Rear Seat Electronics
5. Fueling
6. Instruments (Forward Cockpit)
7. Power Plant Servicing
8. Lower Cockpit Access
9. Loading 20mm Cannon
10. Loading Wing Racks

C

Bibliography

The following books were most helpful in the preparation of the manuscript.

Air Power and the Fight for Khe Sanh, Office of U.S. Air Force History, 1973.

The Douglas Skyraider, by Harry Gann, Profile Publications, 1965.

Douglas Skyraider, by B. R. Jackson, Aero Publishers, Inc., Fallbrook, California, 1969.

Ed Heinemann: Combat Aircraft Designer, by Edward H. Heinemann and Rosario Rausa, Naval Institute Press, Annapolis, 1980.

A History of the Douglas Skyraider AEW.1, British Aviation Research Group, 1974.

McDonnell Douglas Aircraft Since 1920, by René J. Francillon, Putnam, London, 1979.

The United States Air Force in Southeast Asia, edited by Carl Berger, Office of U.S. Air Force History, 1977.

U.S. Navy Aircraft Since 1911, by Gordon Swanborough and Peter M. Bowers, Naval Institute Press, Annapolis, 1976.

The Naval Air War in Vietnam, by Peter Mersky and Norman Polmar, Nautical and Aviation Publishing Company of America, Annapolis, 1981.

The Sea War in Korea, by Malcolm W. Cagle and Frank A. Manson, Naval Institute Press, Annapolis, 1957.

Service Information Summary, Douglas Aircraft Company Souvenir Issue (Naval Aviation 50th Anniversary), January–February 1962.

Though not used directly as source material, the following books concern Skyraiders and Skyraider pilots and are recommended reading:

Escape from Laos, by Dieter Dengler, Presidio Press, San Rafael, California, 1979.

My Secret War, by Richard S. Drury, Aero Publishers, Inc., Fallbrook, California 1975.

Numerous feature articles, factory reports, newspaper stories, and miscellaneous notes were drawn upon in the course of gathering information for this book. Some of the key ones are listed below.

"Skyraider," *Leatherneck*, April 1952.

"Douglas Skyraider," *Aero Digest*, November, 1951.

"The Forgotten Heroes of Korea," by James Michener, *Saturday Evening Post*, 10 May 1952.

"A Saga of Old Rough and Ready—the AD," *Douglas Airview News*, 30 January 1953.

"Farewell to 'Spads'," by Lieutenant Commander A. Doge McFall, *U.S. Naval Institute Proceedings*, April 1965, 54–59.

"Navy Flyers Swear By Old Skyraider Planes," *Los Angeles Times*, 9 May 1965.

"Dogfighting With MiGs," Editorial, *Aviation Week and Space Technology*, 26 July 1965.

"A Pilot Is Down," by Richard Armstrong, *Reader's Digest* (condensation from the *Saturday Evening Post*), August 1966, 42–48.

"How Bernie Fisher Won His Medal," by William D. Feeny, *Air Progress*, May 1967, 42–45.

"An Old Bird Folds Its Wings," by Michael Getler, *Aerospace Technology*, 3 June 1968.

"Skyraider," by Art Cornelius, *Air Classics*, August 1970.

"Skyraiders of No. 849 Squadron," by Arthur Pearcy, Jr., *American Aviation Historical Society Journal*, Fall 1970, Volume 15, Number 3, 151–157.

"Sa Majeste Le Skyraider," by Jean-Michel Lefebvre, *Aviation News*, 10.

"U.S. Air Force and the Medal of Honor," *Air Force Magazine*, September 1970.

"Aging Skyraider Dear to Hearts of Viet Pilots," *Los Angeles Times*, 1 November 1970.

"Ancient 'Spads' Still Sputtering Over Viet," by George McArthur, *Pacific Stars and Stripes*, 11 November 1970.

Skyraider

"Into the Valley of Death," *Air Classics*, September 1972, 19–23.

"Korean War Cruise CVG-4," by Peter Kilduff, *The Hook*, Winter 1978.

Excluding the books mentioned, these documents plus a substantial amount of information not listed but collected while preparing this book have been turned over to the U.S. Naval Aviation History Office in Washington, D.C. for possible use by interested personnel.

Index

Skyraider

Skyraider